MESS
MANAGEMENT

Lessons From a Corporate Hitman

Steve M. Cohen Ed.D.

ISBN
978-1-0880-6515-0 (Paperback)
978-1-0880-6522-8 (eBook)

Table of Contents

Introduction

My many experiences have shown me that nobody gets away with "it" for very long. Whatever "it" is will come out and be dealt with in the end. Whether you are Bernie Madoff or the guy who runs the small business on the street corner, if you are misbehaving, your misbehavior will be exposed. Whether you are an alcoholic, a drug addict, a sex addict, or a ruthless co-worker or boss, the universe takes its revenge and the piper gets paid. That's how it works in life and in business. *Mess Management* is about corporate misbehavior, what happens when it gets exposed, and how it eventually gets fixed.

Corporations and business in general are amoral; they exist to make a profit. The objective is to make money for the shareholders. Period. Even not-for-profit organizations must either make or have money to do the good works specified by their governance. Not-for-profits call it a "fund balance," while the rest call it profits. If morality is to be injected into the mix, it will be done so by people — usually the leaders — choosing to infuse morality and ethical behavior into their business plan and operation. This is, in large part, the basis for the organization's culture.

This book consists of some of the cases I have had over the past 20 or so years. Business war stories are filled with "sex, drugs, and rock'n'roll." They are also stories that, I hope, can accelerate the learning curve for all business owners on what to do, what to avoid doing, the various laws and rules, and how they can be used against you. That is the purpose of the book. As I will say many times, the government, the courts, their laws and rules, and even the court of public opinion is stacked against the business owner and operator.

As a young student, I remember hearing that adversity builds character. That may be true. What I know to be true is that adversity reveals character.

When we find ourselves up against the proverbial wall, our true character is revealed. Will we stand up and do the right thing, or will we deceive, lie, cheat or throw someone under the bus? Will we fix blame or will we fix problems? Sure, our first instinct is fight or flight, depending on our personal bias, but we are not animals who solely rely on instincts. We have the ability to reason. And, when that reason takes hold of us, and we are making choices, our character gets revealed. Can we admit that we were, even momentarily, incompetent or that the job was completely over our head? Do we try the same thing again and expect different results, or do we try something new in our pursuit of a different outcome or solution? Finally, while in pursuit of this change, do we take the shortcut or take advantage of someone or something? Whatever the problem is, what we do shows who we are.

Politics and the media play a very prevalent role in our society as they provide an overarching view. They tell us what we look like to the outsider. I assert they have played a very deleterious role in our lives and in society in general. We see our politicians, every day, trying to talk their way out of what they have behaved their way into. Current and past politicians in positions of power have said that spending levels cannot be sustained and must be reined in, yet they are the ones doing the spending! We see politicians employ tricky accounting methods and then say their programs are affordable. We see the media behaving in a corrupt and dishonest way. They may distort the facts, omit the "other side," and even slander whoever disagrees with them, yet they are honored and glorified as intellectuals and oracles.

Hollywood and Madison Avenue spin reality to portray whatever they wish to portray and sell, regardless of the cost or value. There seems to be a race to the bottom and there is no bottom! Get attention, get the sale, and get ahead at any cost. Is it any wonder we are cynical? I want the Charlie Rangel deal where I don't pay my taxes, and then when I get caught, nothing happens! With role models like these, as powerful and pervasive as they are, how can doing the right thing prevail? You can't argue with success.

With the US and the worldwide economy exposed for the fragile entities that they are and businesses existing on the edge of solvency, can we afford the extra costs associated with morality or ethics? Isn't that a burden? Laws and rules are already very biased against owners and operators of businesses and toward employees and unions. Governments force multiple levels of regulations, and unions impose additional steps or procedures — all adding costs. Should businesses endure more impingements? How much dead weight can we swim with and actually stay afloat? Most owners and operators I know are so focused on the production and performance aspects of their business that anything else—often everything else — is seen as taking them "off line."

Adam Smith, arguably the first economist and the father of modern capitalism, asserted that the efforts and costs associated with putting the customer first ultimately serve the selfish interests of the mercantilist. When the customer is served best, the customer will consume. The true and only underlying motive of the mercantilist is to make money. If, by injecting customer service steps into the equation more money can be made, then the mercantilist will inject those steps and endure those costs. Capitalism civilizes greed just as marriage civilizes sex. Could this notion be expanded to suggest that the efforts expended to inject morality and fairness into the marketplace be rewarded by the marketplace? Is the argument about businesses "going green" really rewarded in the marketplace? Clearly, the marketplace is a very tough place. There are many forces at work that bring out the worst in people. The need to survive often supersedes the need to play fair for most humans.

This is where I come in. My job is to fix the problem when someone doesn't play fair. I do not see myself as any white knight riding in to make things right. I am not the Equalizer, and I am certainly not perfect. I am a business owner as well, but I have a very unique business. For the past 22 years, I have had a business consultancy focused on fixing things, mostly problems related to people. I affectionately call it "mess management." My typical assignment is to come into a business setting and address an allegation. You may ask, "What is an allegation?" An allegation is neither fact nor fiction. It is an assertion or statement made by someone in the business, usually about someone or something that has gone wrong.

If you stop to think about it, an allegation begs to be addressed. In a considerate, just and honorable setting, it must be addressed. Consider it this way: A person (an employee) makes an allegation that something is wrong or someone has done something bad or inappropriate. Maybe a slip hazard exists down the hall representing a danger to anyone who inadvertently walks through it. It could be that someone has done something that has offended or accosted someone. Someone blows a whistle. It must be investigated. To disregard the allegation is to tangibly communicate to the one making the allegation, "You don't count." Conversely, to take it seriously and to conduct a proper investigation clearly communicates that "You count and we (management) care about you." Imagine how you would feel if your boss or co-workers said what you were concerned about was nothing, and you were silly to be worried about it. How would you feel, and what might you do about your concern being minimized or even ignored? The work setting must conduct an investigation of all allegations because, as a matter of common decency, it owes it to its employees. What to do about the situation, once it has been investigated, is another matter that will be addressed later.

We all have different thresholds. The littlest thing can offend some, while others will tolerate way too much. You will see this in two different cases presented later in the book. One woman was invited to lunch by her supervisor and filed a complaint of sexual harassment—just about being invited to lunch. Another woman was forced to perform oral and vaginal sex with her supervisor, over and over again over a period of two years, and she didn't even want him fired, just to stop! There are moral and legal ramifications, as well as liabilities, for employer organizations depending on how they react. Organizations can get in trouble for over-reacting as well as under-reacting. There can be liability for doing too much or too little.

Think about baseball, where the pitcher initiates the action and the catcher ends it. When this happens, the batter asks, "Was it a strike or a ball?"

and it's up to the umpire to decide. In my consultancy, I am the umpire called in by management as an independent third party to call the pitch —to investigate the allegation and to recommend a remedy. A negative allegation is made, and I come in to "get to the bottom of it." My job is to conduct an investigation or inquiry into the allegation. My conclusions fall into one of three categories. I can substantiate the allegation having found it to be true or not substantiate it having found it to be untrue. The third possibility is that I may find that the allegation's truth cannot be determined; therefore, I can neither substantiate nor overturn it.

The investigation is phase one of my typical assignment. I determine what happened to whom and what impact (legally and otherwise) the situation has had on all parties including the organization as a whole. Phase two is to recommend the remedy. This is the "where do we go from here now that we know what happened" step. Once I have substantiated the allegation, I will do something that few consultants do — if appropriate, I will recommend termination. Most consultants will not take this position because by doing so they are taking on legal liability. They will recommend three or four alternatives, termination being one. If the client company chooses to terminate, then it is the company's choice and the consultant dodges the liability. In my opinion, this is a weasel's position. I take a stand. Not only will I recommend termination, I will offer to conduct it, which is phase three. If I were knee deep in legal liability for recommending termination, by conducting it I am up to my ears in legal liability now. The legal term is "acted in reliance." My client can say, "That guy from Kansas City not only said we should fire the employee, he conducted the termination so if there is a problem it must be his." One can see that a huge portion of the legal liability should be on my shoulders.

Phase four, if requested, is to conduct a search for the replacement person that I terminated in phase three. I am qualified to do search work in general, but I have an added expertise to conduct this search in this particular organization because of my activities in phase one and two. I understand the culture of the organization as well as what is does and does not need in the replacement person.

Businesses have the option of a fifth phase as well, which is to act as the interim replacement person while I or someone else conducts the search for the permanent replacement. Phases four and five depend on the choice of the organization's leaders.

Mine is an unusual consultancy. As far as I know, there is no other like it in the country. Few people enjoy putting their hand in a fan. Basically, I become the bomb squad. I either defuse the bomb (the situation) or it goes off, primarily on me! I take the situation out of the corporation's hands. I take it off-line and address it independently of the day-to-day operation of the organization. Few people are prepared to deal with other people who suffer from mental illness or are alcoholics, drug addicts, sex addicts etc. Some people are unhealthy and impaired, and some are not. Some are good people who are just bad matches for the culture of their new boss or company. I am authorized to get the matter and the person in the organization's rear view mirror. Mishandling these kinds of situations, and there are many ways to mishandle them, can get very expensive and even be dangerous. We have read regularly about businesses that have gone under because of it, as well as former employees who have come back with a gun.

While the worst thing that can happen is when one fires someone and that person comes back with a gun, the next worst thing is that he or she comes back with an EEOC or state human rights commission or civil court complaint. In addition, the former employee will always bad-mouth the organization in the marketplace. There is an important legal point here. Legally, the terminated employee can say anything he or she wants about the former employer or the former boss. Anything. It can be outrageous, it doesn't even have to be true, and there is nothing that can be done about it. On the other hand, if the company says anything derogatory about the person (without the person's permission) they have violated that person's confidentiality rights and can be legally held accountable for that violation.

The former employee can own public opinion. My mission and objective is to see that none of these bad things happen. In most states and in the federal system, the terminated employee has two years post termination (that's the statute of limitations) to seek formal redress in any of the three settings indicated above. Would you like, if you were the former employer, to have this fire burning for up to two years? The thing about litigation is that it is slow, public, expensive, and ends in a win/loose. What I do is the opposite; it is fast, private, cheap (by comparison to litigation) and ends in a win/win.

Who do the owner and operator have on their side? They may have a lawyer, but a lawyer can be expensive and really only helpful if he or she is a labor specialist. Lawyers can have a conflict of interest because they get paid more if there is litigation. The owner may have an HR or personnel director. If the organization has less than about 100 employees, they will not typically have an HR director, and if they do, with all due respect to HR folks, they may not be too helpful. The entry level HR person is basically a confidential clerk. Usually this is a $25,000 to $35,000 person who was hired to do payroll and other accounting or administrative duties with HR responsibilities thrown into the mix. These folks usually collect and store the data that will be used in the lawsuit against the employer.

The next level up is a compliance officer. This is a $45,000 to $60,000 person who knows what the law requires with regard to FMLA, the ADA, the Civil Rights Act of 1964, the Pregnancy Leave Act etc. This is a person who usually says to the owner, "You can't do that without violating the law." He or she can be helpful but doesn't typically know his or her limitations. The highest level of HR professional does, at a cost of $90,000 plus, what I call organizational accountability. Owners, boards, and senior management say" what" the organization is going to do and top level HR pros, working close with executives and owners, form the strategy to determine "how" it can be done without breaking laws and rules, and with the full commitment and engagement of employees.

Small businesses, those with less than about 100 employees, don't have much help. Since they make up the majority of all business driving the economy, they are critically important. If they are profitable, and their employees know they are profitable, they are very vulnerable to being taken advantage of by predatory type employees. There exists in every work group a small percentage of employees who are disengaged and actively working against their employers. They have a wide variety of reasons for being disengaged. Some are understandable, but none are really acceptable. They need to be turned to be reengaged (working with their employers), and focused on management's mission, vision and values or they need to be extricated.

It's not that I enjoy firing people. In fact, in 22 years of doing this work, I have only had to terminate a few. What I do instead is get people "off" of what they want and "on" to what is in their best interest. I get them out of "mad" and into problem solving as quickly as possible. This is the breakthrough. They want to get their job back and for things to return to normal. However, that is not going to happen so I help them understand that while this job is gone, their whole career isn't over. I operate on the premise that, in most cases, people can learn from this situation and make improvements for the next one. Some people are simply a mismatch for their employer. They were succeeding under their old boss only to find themselves failing under the new one. While they may be objectionable to the new boss, they were perfectly acceptable to the previous one. There is no legal provision to terminate someone for being objectionable, but, at the same time, a new employer should have the right to decide who is in his or her employment.

I can help you with situations like this and a myriad of others. Granted, it is an unusual field, and you would be right to wonder not only why I do this kind of work but also how I prepared for it. Let me assure you that my educational background, personal experiences, and personality have made me ideally suited for it.

Educationally, my focus has been a combination of human behavior and business management. I have an undergraduate degree from the University of Kansas in social work with an emphasis in juvenile probation. The plan was to work with juvenile delinquents and help them turn their lives around. Even before I finished my field placement, I realized that even though I possessed the heart of a social worker, it was not my calling.

It so happened that during that four-year period, I had three independent businesses all running simultaneously. Not only did I make a lot of money, I found I really liked business situations and problem solving. In addition to the businesses, I had my classes, my campus politics . . . and all the typical activities and problems of undergrads. I found that I could juggle many things and keep most of the balls in the air. I could handle the pressure.

A few years later, I attended graduate school at Central Michigan University and obtained a masters degree with an emphasis in management and supervision. I was working, married, and even became a father during that time — still juggling. Post-masters and working in hospital administration, I then completed a year-long certification program in healthcare and labor relations with the University of Pennsylvania's Wharton School of Business.

The continued pursuit of my interest in human behavior and business led me to obtaining a Doctorate in Educational Psychology with an emphasis in industrial behavior from Northern Illinois University. My area of study centered on what makes people learn, why they work, and how to get them to do both at a higher level.

Eventually, I attended DePaul University's School of Law's program, Alternative Dispute Resolution, and became a certified mediator. I have never acted as a formal mediator because a formal mediator acts as an independent third party working with two disputants. I am not independent as I work only for management, business owners, and operators or boards. I call what I do "recovery" because the goal is to recover my client's position while avoiding litigation and unnecessary expenses.

My background has enabled me to understand human and business behavior. People are very predictable and once you know where they are likely to go, they can be headed off at the pass. In the 1970's, Elizabeth Kubler-Ross wrote her seminal work, *On Death and Dying*. It was fascinating to learn that there are five distinct steps associated with the grieving process and finally accepting death. I studied that book closely and generalized from it that there are similar steps associated in dealing with and finally accepting the death of a job. Getting people to and through the five steps through mediation techniques is one of my skills.

Even my childhood prepared me to become a mess manager and actually like it! My parents were divorced when I was seven years old and that was the start of multiple moves to multiple family configurations for me, a kid who liked challenges and was somewhat rebellious. After changing homes a few times, my mother eventually got custody of me and remarried. My step- dad was an orthopedic surgeon who was the epitome of tough. He actually did not like me that much, but he did take me seriously and prepared me to be an independent and productive adult. I admired his work ethic and focus on preparation and accuracy. From him, I also learned to, when necessary, take a stand regardless of the consequences. I will always be appreciative of his influence in my life. He often referred to me as a hard-boiled egg because I got tougher instead of softer under pressure. He was right and that tendency has served me well in my consultancy.

Through my step-dad and others, I learned the lessons needed to be what I am and be successful at what I do even if it doesn't make me friends. I once asked Patrick Geschwind, one of my close friends and business partners, "Why do people take an immediate dislike to me?" He told me that they were just saving time! Even though we were just joking around, what I do doesn't always make me popular and I can handle that. I do my job as humanely as possible as I still have a social worker's heart, but I stay focused on the issue and its resolution.

It is my hope that *Mess Management* will not only entertain you but also prepare you to deal with very difficult business situations. While the names have been changed, all cases in the book represent situations that not only can, but probably will, come up in your business. Use the information to help try and solve issues in-house. If you find they can't be fixed without outside intervention, I have another solution for you. Call me.

Chapter 1

Sexual Harassment: The Credit Union Mess

This was a fascinating multi-dimensional case. It started out as a straightforward sexual harassment case but, as they often do, it mushroomed into something quite a bit bigger. I was originally contacted by the CEO of a 65 million dollar credit union affiliated with a federal agency based on the East coast. Called to the corporate offices, I was asked to conduct an investigation of several allegations of sexual harassment made by a female employee against the male CIO (chief information officer).

I questioned the CEO, Joan, about the credit union's sexual harassment prevention policy, its experience with the policy, practices, organizational structure, and relationship with its board of directors, gathering information that would give me an overview of the organization. Joan had been with the credit union for 10 years with her last five as its CEO. She was a CPA by training.

It appeared to me that Joan and her board had a negative, or at least a strange relationship. She told me that she was rarely invited to attend board meetings and usually found out what the board discussed by reading it in the meeting minutes. I insisted that if I were hired, I would be granted an audience with the board, as I wanted to have direct access to the board to make my report. I insisted on this audience not only because I heard this little voice in the back of my head saying something was weird here, but also because sometimes the leader of an organization can be a part of the problem. He or she can directly or indirectly enable the misbehavior to occur and/or continue. If Joan were a part of the problem, I didn't want to be let go and my report thrown into the circular file, never to be read or seen again. She wasn't happy with my request, but she agreed.

Before I go into the case, it will be helpful to understand the law and what is expected of an organization as it relates to sexual harassment. The definition of sexual harassment is deceivingly simple. It is "unwelcome, unsolicited, and unreciprocated behavior of a sexual nature." The law is clear. If sexual harassment has happened in the workplace, there is a violation of one of the elements of the Civil Rights Act of 1964. However, personal interpretation of sexual harassment makes this "clear" law complicated. What is behavior of a sexual nature? Could be anything. It could be inappropriate touching, but then what kind of touching is inappropriate? Is touching a person's arm or shoulder inappropriate? Usually not but for some or in some circumstances, it could be. Is touching a woman's breast or buttocks at work inappropriate? It usually is, but in some circumstances it may have been an accident and acceptable to the person touched. Behavior of a sexual nature could be jokes told between people, pictures or "pin up" type posters on the walls of the workplace, leering, or gestures. The reality is that it could be almost anything.

This leads into another complicated question: Was the behavior unwelcome? If the behavior was of a sexual nature but welcomed, then there was no sexual harassment. Yet, there is actually a situation where welcomed behavior of a sexual nature could still be sexual harassment. What about behavior that was welcomed and acceptable yesterday, but not welcomed and unacceptable the next? What about behavior that was not welcomed by one person, but the same behavior was welcomed by someone else? One can see that the situation gets complicated fast.

There are several other "problems" with the definition. One of the most important questions is: How is the behavior to be judged? This one has an interesting answer. When judging the behavior, the law requires the following question to be asked: Would a reasonable woman find the behavior to be offensive? The question is not would a reasonable man or a reasonable person find the behavior to be offensive. The salient question is would a reasonable woman find the behavior to be offensive. If the answer is yes and the behavior was unwelcome, unsolicited and unreciprocated behavior of a sexual nature, you probably have sexual harassment.

It is important to note that sexual harassment manifests itself in the workplace in three ways. There is quid pro quo sexual harassment, sexual harassment by sexual favoritism, and sexual harassment by hostile environment. Quid pro quo is a Latin word that means "this for that." We do quid pro quos all the time. For example, you go to the store and exchange money for product. Nothing wrong with that. In a context of sexual harassment, it becomes: You do a sexual favor for me, and I will do something for you. Sexual harassment by sexual favoritism is very similar. It looks like this: You do a sexual favor for me, and I will give you the favored shift, approval to attend the seminar you want to attend, or give you the job/raise you are seeking. Sexual harassment by hostile environment is a bit more complicated and the most prevalent in the workplace. It is behavior of a sexual nature that is less direct or obvious as it is behavior that creates a hostile environment. Even though it may be less threatening, it is sexual harassment just the same.

There is one more distinction in the law that you should know both for self-preservation, as well as for following this case. If quid pro quo sexual harassment or sexual harassment by sexual favoritism occurs just one time, it is sexual harassment with all the penalties and costs that go with it. If hostile work environment sexual behavior occurs just once, it is not sexual harassment. It may be tacky, unwelcome, and inappropriate, but if it occurs just once, it is not sexual harassment. In order to have sexual harassment by hostile environment, the behavior must occur in a pattern. Anything more than once is considered a pattern. Let's put this into a concrete example: Joe is the office prankster. He tells Lora a sexually oriented and off-color joke. Lora is offended and tells him not to tell her any more of those jokes. If Joe stops, there is no sexual harassment, but if he continues, he has overridden her objections and persisted in unwelcome behavior of a sexual nature. Thus, we have sexual harassment.

It's also important to know that even if the employer organization has completed comprehensive sexual harassment prevention, at the point of receiving an allegation that someone thinks he or she has been the victim of sexual harassment, the company takes on new liability. The law requires the employer to conduct a thorough and timely investigation. Thorough means thorough — everyone related to the allegation needs to be interviewed. Timely means the investigation must start within 72 hours of management receiving notice. There is no provision in the law for how long an investigation can last, but it must start within 72 hours of the company getting notice of an allegation. The bottom line is that the employer organization must react in a thorough and timely manner. Sexual harassment situations are ones where the employer organization can get in more trouble by under-reacting than by over-reacting. The Department of Labor and the state human rights commissions feel that employers cannot do too much to protect employees, but they can do too little. And, if they do too little, they invite great liability.

In recent years, the US Supreme Court ruled that because sexuality is so pervasive in American culture and sexual harassment in the workplace is illegal, if an employer organization *has not* conducted comprehensive sexual harassment prevention for their employees and the organization receives or is notified of a sexual harassment allegation which is then investigated and substantiated, the employer organization, not the harasser, is held accountable. If, on the other hand, the employer organization *has* conducted comprehensive sexual harassment prevention up to the point of the allegation, the employer organization is held harmless and the perpetrator is the one who is held accountable. If the employer organization has conducted comprehensive sexual harassment prevention, they are essentially judgment proof. But, if they have not conducted comprehensive sexual harassment prevention, it is very easy to beat that organization in a lawsuit.

The definition of comprehensive sexual harassment prevention should also be made clear. My definition is doing most or all of the following:

- Having and distributing a sexual harassment prevention and zero tolerance policy to all staff
- Conducting sexual harassment prevention training for all present employees
- Providing sexual harassment prevention training to all future employees as part of their new hire orientation
- Providing a constant reminder of the policy by placing a poster or reminder on employee bulletin boards or web sites
- Providing an intermittent reminder by providing a "paycheck stuffer" two times a year
- A mid-management commitment to zero tolerance of sexual harassment

Remember that because sexuality is so pervasive in American culture and because sexual harassment is illegal in the workplace, the employer organization must take all reasonable steps to prevent it. If an employer organization sets the above six hurdles in place and an employee still chooses to commit sexual harassment, why should the employer be held accountable? The offending employee clearly is going against the employer's policy and should be held accountable personally.

Keeping the legal aspects in mind, back to the case. When I get to town, I start with the person who hires me (usually the leader, the CEO or board chair) to gain an insight into his or her view of "what has gone wrong" and the various elements of the allegations. The person hiring me will give me his or her take on the characters of the alleged victim and perpetrator. With regard to the perpetrator, I always ask, "Does it seem (to you) that doing what has been alleged to have occurred is a part of that person's character and reputation?" I then ask about the alleged victim's character and reputation. I am seeking insight from the person hiring me regarding the credibility of both parties. I am also seeking the level of connectedness of the leader to his or her people and their work lives. It is not unusual to find a great gulf between what the top leader thinks and the reality "in the trenches." Often, there are problems other than just the ones that brought me into the organization.

What I found in this case was that Joan (the CEO) believed that the alleged perpetrator, Tom (the CIO), was a competent and valuable part of her management team. She thought the allegations could be possible but that they were a bit overblown. She felt that many of the young girls (her word choice — very revealing) regularly wore clothes that were inappropriate for work. Joan thought the choice of dress, quite often, was too sexy and informal. She told me that she often would have to reprimand the staff directly, and one time she even had to send a girl home to change into something more professional. According to Joan, the girls usually got what they wanted or at least deserved. Wow! With an attitude like this, I was a bit surprised I was even hired to investigate. I started to think things were really bad there.

After I have a leader's overview of the allegations and a perspective on the people and situations involved, I always go to the person making the allegation for his or her side of the story. This is always step two. This is a crucial step because if things are mishandled here, liability can explode and things can get really bad. There is a tenet in management that I try to follow: "Never make bigger messes through your intervention than existed prior to your jumping in." The liability to this company already existed because they had not done comprehensive sexual harassment prevention, and they had missed their 72-hour start point for the investigation.

So, we have an organization that had not conducted comprehensive sexual harassment prevention and a CEO who demonstrated a lack of sensitivity. What happens next? After I get the lay of the land from a CEO or leader, I always go the person who made the allegation—the victim, who in this case was Sarah. She was a teller who was seeking a promotion to the information services department as she had completed her college degree in computer science. Speaking with her next was critical. Without being judgmental, without taking a stand or even hinting at a stand, I must get her story next. Think about what it would say to talk to the alleged perpetrator before speaking with the alleged victim. First of all, it could set the alleged victim on the defensive because my view could be clouded by what the alleged perpetrator said. She is the alleged victim, and I want to communicate warmth and get a complete picture of what happened from her first.

Notice that I have used the term "her" for the alleged victim and "him" for the alleged perpetrator. It could happen the other way with a woman sexually harassing a male. Sexual harassment can also occur between people of the same gender. Most often though, it occurs between a man and a woman with the man acting as the perpetrator and the woman as the victim. When it is not a male harassing a female, the question becomes: "Would a reasonable *person* find the behavior to be offensive?

My next step is to interview the alleged perpetrator. I now have both sides so I start talking with potential witnesses. These potential witnesses are usually identified by the two people I have previously interviewed, the victim and perpetrator. I always ask each to provide the names of any other employee who might be able to shed any light on the matter or could corroborate anything previously alleged or asserted.

So what happened? Here is where it got juicy. There were six different allegations:

1. The rabbit ears incident: At a credit union sponsored Halloween party for the staff, Sarah came dressed in a rabbit costume that had big pointed rabbit ears. Tom approached her, touched the ears and said, "I just wanted to be able to say I touched your tips." There were no witnesses, and Tom denied making the statement. He did acknowledge that he noticed her in the costume and told me all he said to her was, "I like your tips." Sarah told her friend, Kristen, as well as her immediate supervisor, Bob, about the incident. These two individuals (witnesses) were quite convincing in their report of the incident. It was interesting and perhaps significant that Tom was alleged to have said the words, "*I just wanted to be able to say* I touched your tips." I discovered that almost all of Tom's inappropriate behavior revolved around locker room or street corner crass talk rather than overt actions. I believed the allegation had merit. The target, Sarah, had credibility, as did

her friend and her supervisor. This behavior, coupled with other behaviors that I soon discovered, amounted to sexual harassment by hostile work environment.

2. The cell phone camera incident: Continuing to cross the line, Tom took a picture of Sarah from the front, neck to waist. Kristen actually saw the picture being taken and expressed her disapproval. She demanded that he delete the picture. Tom told Kristen that he would delete the picture but would not show her that it was deleted from the camera phone. Then, he denied even taking any picture of Sarah's breasts when I interviewed him. Both Sarah and Kristen asserted that Tom did take the picture and refused to delete it. Joan reported to me that Tom admitted to her that he did take the picture. This allegation is substantiated. The real mistake here was Tom's refusal to delete the picture. It was possible that the picture was taken inadvertently. The situation presented an opportunity to simply apologize. Tom could have demonstrated sincere contrition, proved that the picture was deleted, and the incident could have been closed. Instead, the victim was left wondering what purpose this picture would serve, who would see it, etc. This behavior, coupled with other behavior, constituted sexual harassment by hostile work environment.

3. Denied promotional opportunities: Sarah and Tom were discussing a promotional opportunity, the manager of product support position within the IS department. Tom told her that the position required overnight travel. She said she understood and had no problems with that requirement of the new job. He further advised Sarah that, during that overnight travel, she would have to share a hotel room and bed with him! She informed him in no uncertain terms that his suggestion was unacceptable and unwelcome. She told me that she told Tom that any part of him that touched her would be cut off and sent home in a box! She did not get the job.

A second opportunity arose for a position as the assistant product support manager in the IS department. Alan, the product support manager, recruited Sarah. He advocated for Sarah to get the position on three or more separate instances with his boss, Tom. Alan was very clear with me that Tom continuously refused to grant his request to hire Sarah. He said that Tom provided very lame excuses or reasons why Sarah could not be selected for the position. The final reason Tom provided for rejecting Sarah's candidacy was that there might be a problem with Sarah's compensation in the new position being higher than the compensation paid to her fiancée who also worked in the IS department. Tom denied the allegation indicating that Sarah did not get either position because she was not qualified for either one. Upon review of the qualifications for the first manager position, Sarah did not appear qualified. However, for the assistant classification, she appeared to be fully qualified. The first allegation, the assertion that the position required overnight travel and that Sarah would have to share a room and bed with Tom constituted quid pro quo sexual harassment. The second allegation, that her salary could not be allowed to exceed that of her fiancé's compensation, constituted gender bias, which is also illegal.

On an additional note, a male was eventually hired for the assistant manager's position. He lasted three months and left. With the position open again, Alan immediately went back to Tom and advocated for Sarah to be offered the job. He argued that Sarah was qualified, was his choice, and available. Tom advised him that she could apply again to which Tom argued that there was no need to restart the search process and incur the expense in money and time all over again. This argument was rejected. Alan told me that he did not wish to expose Sarah to the humiliation associated with going through the search process again. It was very understandable that Sarah would not wish to expose herself to the search process again either. This second incident served to humiliate Sarah. It also served to marginalize Alan and his judgment, as it had always been his choice to select Sarah. It sent a negative and chilling message throughout the organization as well — that management could make capricious and arbitrary decisions, no rational needed.

My recommendation was for the credit union to immediately offer the position to Sarah with apologies for the past mistakes and offer apologies to Alan for the treatment he had endured.

4. Unsubstantiated comments to Sarah: Tom made crude sexual comments to Sarah and reminded her that he, as the CIO, controlled the employment and promotional opportunities of her fiancé. He asserted that if she wanted to protect her fiancé, she could do so by being more "friendly." Tom denied ever saying anything crude or inappropriate to Sarah and asserted that he never threatened her fiancé's position or promotional opportunities. These statements were not made in front of witnesses. There was not enough evidence to substantiate these allegations, yet there was also no information to contradict them. The credibility of the parties was left as the deciding factor. Sarah's credibility, in my opinion, was far superior to that of Tom's. If true, this allegation represented or constituted sexual harassment of the worst kind: the acceptance of the marginalization and denigration of women simply because they are women.

5. Substantiated racist and sexual comments about Sarah and women in general: On several occasions, Tom made sexually, racially insensitive and inappropriate statements about female staff or women in general. In my many interviews with him, Tom denied ever making any such comments. My investigation substantiated the allegations because several managers and line staff indicated direct personal experience with Tom when he made crude and inappropriate sexual and racial comments about female staff, including Sarah and women in general. There were smoke breaks on many occasions, and over a period of many months and years, when he made the comments. The incidents represented reprehensible role modeling and wholly unacceptable management practice. This behavior undermined the values of decency, professionalism and safety. They also undermined any other efforts the credit union might have been taking to become employee centered.

6. Alleged overt actions: There was a statement made to me that Tom unsnapped the bra of a female staff person sometime in the recent past. Several women had knowledge about the incident, but no one would say that it happened to them, just that they had heard about it. This allegation could not be substantiated. It is important to know that when an allegation like the one in this case is investigated, there will usually be many more related issues that will surface. Some will be able to be substantiated and some, like the bra allegation, will not. Either way, I promise you that they will be there.

Know that Tom was given a chance to respond to each of the allegations. His behavior met the definition of sexual harassment by hostile environment, by quid pro quo, and by sexual favoritism. While I did not think Tom was a sexual predator because all of his substantiated behavior had been talk, his behavior was illegal as he had committed sexual harassment.

The credit union's board and Joan incurred significant liability by "sitting on the allegations." Joan had also incurred liability for not detecting the harassment earlier. Again, the way the law works in this situation, the employer organization can get in more trouble for underreacting then for overreacting. In the eyes of the EEOC, the employer cannot do too much to protect employees, but it can do too little. So far the credit union had done too little. I urged the board and the CEO not to continue to underreact now that it had the results of the investigation. If Sarah had an opportunistic bias, she could have filed a lawsuit or an EEOC complaint. My estimation was that a six-figure (or greater) case against the credit union could have been won. I urged Tom's termination.

Throughout the process of investigating the sexual harassment allegations, I discovered several other matters that not only needed to be reported, but seriously called for corrective action. I learned that the credit union's processes were organized to be convenient to management. It was obvious to me, and many staff personnel, that they should be set up to be customer centered. All applicable systems must be designed so that customers feel they are an honored priority. To do this, the organization must also become employee centered. All applicable systems must be designed in a way that line employees and first-line supervisors also feel they are valued and a priority. These two notions are not mutually exclusive; they can and must coexist. I suggested the following changes to help the organization "walk the talk."

1. Several departments had daily and weekly reports that existed ostensibly for the CEO and the EVP to monitor performance. In reality, they did monitor performance, but they also undermined trust because they were perceived to be "big brother/big sister watching," and they consumed considerable time that could be spent serving members. The opportunity costs of all the report writing undermined customer servicing.

Recommendations: Reduce reporting demands on staff. Mid-level managers can/should be held responsible to monitor day-to-day performance via a variety of obvious and unobtrusive measures like obtaining regular feedback from members. Senior management currently spent an inordinate amount of time devouring reports of line activities and then proceeded to micromanage the mid-managers. Senior management should spend its time on strategic matters and high level problem solving/problem avoidance like obtaining more accessibility to the services of the credit union, assuring that all departmental processes are established and systematized, and/or deciding on the options and priorities for growth and new business.

2. There were far too few systems available for line-level staff to solve routine and chronic problems. First-line managers were relegated to followers, not leaders. The CEO and the VP's to some extent, and the EVP to a great extent, micromanaged staff by acting as firefighters. They said, "This is how to do it," and they said, "Do it my way." On top of this, they were inconsistent in the directions they provided. One week the answer was X; the next week the answer to the same question could be Y.

Recommendations: Empower and engage the high performers group. This is a newly assembled group of recognized achievers. They and others who are line-level staff need to be empowered to engage in structured problem solving. First-line supervisors need to be empowered to prioritize the recommendations made by the line staff. Then, senior management needs to allocate resources to implement the recommended changes.

3. There are severe "NIH" problems. NIH stands for "not invented here." If the EVP, the CEO or occasionally one of the VP's comes up with an idea, it is shoved through rapidly. Often it is implemented so quickly that it engenders unnecessary negativity with the line staff and the first-line supervisors. If the first-line supervisors or line staff come up with an idea, the senior group stalls, demands more data, and throws up barriers and roadblocks. This serves to demotivate staff. Examples include: A first-line supervisor selected and recruited a qualified person from the line level. He or she was precluded from promoting this person. This example was detailed in the sexual harassment portion of this report. Another example was one of the tech staff fielded concerns from the line staff that porn and spam were invading their email. He researched for a solution and came up with a software fix that would cost $600. He was told to go back into the marketplace and identify three more fix options. At that time, there weren't as many options as today so he could not find three more options and no fix was approved. Later that year, the CIO came up with a software solution himself and paid $3,000 for it.

    Recommendations: Empower all staff to think and engage in problem solving. Require reasonable cost benefit analysis.

4. Departmental operations needed to be systematized and training in the "credit union way" needed to be established and provided. There were no meaningful structured systems in place for departmental orientation and training. When new hires were brought in, they typically got placed with someone for a day or two. There was no training, no orientation, and no break-in period. This situation caused the new hires to rely on insufficient information and their own devices or ideas to answer questions.

The employee was expected to take that information, or lack thereof, as how business was done at the credit union. It did not inspire confidence on anyone's part. Good people were using poor systems which produced inconsistencies, a bad image, spotty quality, and frustration. Good people using good systems will always produce consistent quality and success. Even mediocre people using good systems will produce good results. Look at McDonalds as an example and model.

Recommendations: There was a new staff trainer. She seemed extremely well-suited in terms of personality and technical background in credit unions. She should be directed to prioritize the development of an orientation and training process department by department. She could start with a content expert in each department and develop a manual specifying the "credit union way" for dealing with the most commonly asked questions, the production processes employed in the department, and the scripts for different problems.

5. The current system of compensation needed to be abandoned, and the organization needed to install a performance appraisal system. The current system for compensation was totally ineffective and the source of much dissatisfaction within the staff. It could be "gamed" and new hires were even instructed by their peers *and supervisors* regarding how to "game" it. For those who chose not to take advantage of the system but rather ignore it due to its ineptness, no raises were granted. I spoke with several people who had received no raise for several years running.

Recommendation: Scrap the current system and install an effective performance appraisal system. I offered to provide a model system, which has been very successful in many of my other client organizations.

6. The dress code needed to be revised. This was a source of dissatisfaction in the organization as it was applied capriciously and inconsistently. Large women whose cleavage was showing were

not held accountable but thin, young women in the same situation got humiliated and sent home to change outfits.

Recommendation: Charge the high achievers group to develop a new set of dress code standards. This could include a Friday dress-down day. The group recommends the plan, and the first-line managers edit and provide "check balance," and then present it to senior management for approval. Once approved, allow the first-line managers to monitor and uphold the new code. Senior management should not engage staff on this matter.

7. The physical environment needed to be upgraded as it suggested chaos and little concern for esthetics. The home office was dreary, depressing, and cluttered in its appearance. Little could be done about the architecture, but much could be done to set standards for appearance.

Recommendation: Charge the high achievers group to develop a comprehensive list of all corrections that are needed. This group could specify that a hall and room need painting, exposed wire needs to be relocated, stacks of brochures need to be stored in a different location rather than cluttering the conference room etc. Once the list is complete, the first-line managers could prioritize the list and present a plan and schedule to senior management for approval of the allocation of resources.

There was one more set of findings and accompanying recommendations. This was, on the surface, a bit hard for me but after consideration, I realized that ethically it must be done. I discovered a very close relationship between Joan, and her EVP, Robert. I discovered that Joan and Robert attended graduate school together while getting masters degrees in accounting. Robert, like Joan, was a CPA, and they both spent social time together along with their spouses. There was no sexuality or inappropriateness in their relationship that I detected or even suspected; they were just very close friends and colleagues. Joan recruited him five years ago to join her as the EVP at the credit union when she was promoted to CEO. There was no EVP position prior to his recruitment; Joan created the position to be her number two.

When referring to Robert, to call him a jerk would be an understatement. His management style was the most dictatorial and mean-spirited that I had ever witnessed. He was a yeller and a curser, and he would literally throw reports back in a manager's face or across the room in disgust. He was a large person, and it was reported to me that he seemed to love intimidating others. I was told he behaved like an adolescent bully in a schoolyard with no teachers within a mile radius. He didn't display any of this to me, but I received report after report of Robert's antics. I spoke to all of Robert's subordinates and was provided with the names and contact information of former employees who were his alleged victims.

What I discovered was shocking. Five current employees under the age of 40 were seeing doctors and taking medication for anxiety and stress. One employee, the VP of the mortgage section was taken out of the building on a stretcher because he suffered a heart attack on duty due to the pressure associated with dealing with Robert and trying to meet his performance expectations. This man was under 50 years of age! I questioned the VP and his staff and learned that the mortgage department provided members with funds for new mortgages. This was a very profitable department for the credit union. The staff recognized their importance to the credit union's profitability and also recognized how serious the mortgage documents were as they were regulated by government agency. Not only did they take their work seriously, they were proud of it. So, this VP is taken away on a stretcher to a hospital and then sent home for a 90-day recovery with orders to stay away from work — bed rest only. When he left work, he told me there were approximately 30 mortgage applications in the department's pipeline. Upon his return from medical leave, there were over 60 applications in the pipeline, and the staff was overwhelmed. When he saw what his staff was having to do, he asked his boss, Robert, why he didn't get them more help. Robert's response was, "I wanted to see if they would sink or swim." My thought was that he was trying to see who else could get a heart attack!

With the department being so profitable and the work being so exact, mistakes must be avoided. I thought the credit union would have been encouraged to get the mortgage department staffed up to get the work out the door and the profits rolling in. Instead, the credit union, at the direct hands of Robert and the indirect hands of Joan (she protects the EVP as complaints are made therefore approving of his methods and behaviors) stressed staff to the point of seeing doctors, taking medications, and getting heart attacks. Beautiful.

I reported to the board that, in my opinion, the pressure the CEO and EVP brought to bear on the staff was beyond anything that should be tolerated in a business setting. I postulated that if the credit union were to be investigated by the state human rights commission or the EEOC, there would be six or even seven figure fines leveled against it for victimization of staff. I further reported that the interpersonal environment at the credit union was toxic in that the two individuals, Joan and Robert, consistently displayed inappropriate and unprofessional behavior, and that morale was low and turnover very high. The technical environment was also deficient in that the compensation system was counterproductive, the orientation and training process virtually non-existent, and the one system for employee level involvement in problem solving was brand new after being nonexistent for years. At this point, the outside investigation had substantiated the dissatisfaction of the staff and the sexual harassment perpetrated by Tom. The board should be alarmed at the depth and breadth of the malpractice exhibited by the three individuals mentioned above and must take action.

In the end, the board acknowledged the malpractice exhibited by Joan, Robert and Tom. They hired me to terminate the three leaders, which I gladly did. No three deserved to be gone more than those three. I was hired to act as the interim CEO while the board conducted its own search for the new CEO. Once hired, the new CEO did not replace the EVP position and promoted a highly qualified internal person to become the new CIO.

I stayed on about four months as the acting CEO while the board conducted their search. I will readily acknowledge that I knew nothing about running a credit union. I had no experience as a banker, but in this case none was needed. The VPs in each of the various departments were content experts, and they were empowered by me to operate their departments, as they needed to in order to be effective and stay in compliance with the applicable rules and laws. What was needed was leadership and efforts to humanize the environment. My job was to empower and enable people to do and be their best. Many acted like whipped dogs, and it takes time to come out of that, time for them to emerge from such a disheartening experience. I was able to start the process of taking the credit union from a place that was unsafe to safe, from dictatorial to participative, from chauvinistic to gender fair, and from unprofessional to professional. It was all very exciting and uplifting to see the organization transform.

I wish I could say that everything turned out well in the end. The truth is, I don't think it did. The new CEO was not really a people person (which was what the staff desperately needed and I would have recruited). He was a technocrat who was more of a banker than a leader. He wasn't an ogre, but he wasn't the accessible, friendly type either.

During my four months, I also discovered that the board had established a scholarship fund supposedly for the staff, but they were using it to provide scholarships for board members' own kids. I also figured out that they were holding board meetings on cruise ships and in Florida. This is the board of a not-for-profit based in the Northeast. I advised that what they were doing in these two instances was unethical, perhaps illegal, and that they should stop. I was thanked for my work and opinions and promptly terminated. It was very frustrating taking phone calls from VP's and others who lamented my departure and reported that things I had started were being discarded by the new CEO. I was in no position to help them, but I told them I would be glad to provide testimony in their lawsuits if they were wrongfully terminated. Boo. Hiss.

Management Lessons

1. The first objective of management is to never make a bigger mess through your intervention than existed prior to your jumping in. This is similar to the oath that physicians take to "do no harm." The role of management is to fix and organize things. If

management makes things worse through its steps and choices, then it's producing no value.

2. This chapter spent a great deal of time on the subject of sexual harassment. The legal definition of sexual harassment is unwelcomed, unsolicited, and unreciprocated behavior of a sexual nature. Sexual harassment can occur in three scenarios: quid pro quo —literally translated as "this for that;" sexual harassment by sexual favoritism; and sexual harassment by hostile work environment.

3. The US Supreme Court in recent years made a very balanced and appropriate decision relating to sexual harassment in the workplace. The ruling specified that business organizations that conduct "comprehensive sexual harassment prevention" are very difficult to sue. On the contrary, business organizations that fail to conduct "comprehensive sexual harassment prevention" are very easy to sue. My suggestion for comprehensive sexual harassment prevention consists of the following six steps:

    • Having and distributing a sexual harassment prevention and zero tolerance policy to all staff
    • Conducting sexual harassment prevention training for all present employees
    • Providing sexual harassment prevention training to all future employees as part of their new hire orientation
    • Providing a constant reminder of the policy by placing a poster or reminder on employee bulletin boards or web sites
    • Providing an intermittent reminder by providing a "paycheck stuffer" two times a year
    • A mid-management commitment to zero tolerance of sexual harassment

If a company takes all of these steps, then they cannot be held accountable if an employee chooses to go "over" the steps and sexually harass another employee.

4. Should an allegation of sexual harassment occur within a company, new liability for the company has just emerged. The US Department of Labor requires the company to conduct, or get someone outside the company to conduct, a thorough and timely investigation. Thorough means thorough. In other words, the investigation must include all parties to the allegation. Timely means the investigation must start within 72 hours of the company getting notice of the allegation.

5. In this chapter, I suggested that a business systematize and formalize as many of its activities as possible. The lowest level of organizational or business behavior is a business practice. My recommendation is that the business owner/operator elevate from practice to policy. At a minimum, every business that has employees should have an employee policy and procedure manual. This manual provides clarification and clarity regarding regular business activities. The way the law works is that employees cannot be legally held accountable to follow practices, but can be held legally accountable to follow policies. A policy is just a practice that has been formally presented as an expectation of management. In addition to the legal ramifications, the more management systematizes its behaviors and expectations, the more predictability and comfort is provided to employees. If there are no systems in place, then management and employees must rely on mood and attitude.

6. If good people are using good systems, then the results will always be good. If good people are using mediocre systems, or the reverse and mediocre people are using good systems, there may be frustrations, but results will still usually be good. However, if mediocre people are using mediocre systems, the results will usually be mediocre. Look at McDonald's as an example. McDonald's is consistently rated as one of the best-run companies in the world. It is systematized to the maximum. You can always count on the product being good whether it is produced in the Midwest, the Northeast or in the Orient. Who operates McDonald's at the store

level? Kids. Who supervises McDonald's at the store level? Kids who have hung around long enough to be promoted. Mediocre people using exceptional systems can produce exceptional results

Chapter 2

Avoiding Race-Based Discrimination: The High Performance Misfit

In this case, there was a high performance organization that hired an African-American woman, Corinne. She interviewed well, was articulate, and her resume indicated she had the qualifications to excel at the position. However, it turned out that she did not excel at the job in this high performance organization, and I was brought in to extricate her.

One of the things I always try to help my clients achieve is a "high performance" organization. A common question is: How is this achieved? A more important question is: What is a high performance organization? I help my clients become a high performance organization through human resources system developments like job descriptions, performance appraisals, policy manuals, and compensation plans, Additionally, I help them become high performance through personnel changes. You may be tempted to think a high performance organization is achieved through improving efficiency — running lean and mean comes to mind. No doubt this is an important part of the equation. However, as a business psychologist, I see the employees as the bigger part of the mix.

Research by the Gallagher Organization has suggested that only 25 percent of the typical work force is engaged. This means that only this fraction of the employees in the typical organization are truly in tune with management's mission, vision, and values. These employees are the core group who can always be counted upon to produce and make things happen. They train the new people, carry the owner's banner, and stick up for the company through bad times.

The second group, representing about 15 percent of the typical work group, is disengaged. These are the ones who actively work against management. These employees are disgruntled, negative, and act to undermine the organization. They will throw cold water on any idea and attempt to take new employees under their wings and corrupt them as quickly as possible. The last to convert to a new way of doing things and the first to complain, this group is made up of individuals who are usually very technically competent. The problem is that interpersonally they are incompetent. They get passed over for promotions but get to keep their jobs due to their technical knowledge. Management puts up with them, but if they actually knew how much undermining and damage this group caused, management would readily and willingly drop them.

The third group of employees is the 60 percent who are neither engaged nor disengaged. They do their jobs but usually not well enough or poor enough to be recognized. This group does not live to work, but rather works to live, usually doing their jobs and heading on home. Perhaps you could call them underachievers. They underachieve, in part, because they are not engaged but also perhaps because they have not been recognized and encouraged to achieve. People usually live up to or down to the expectations others have for them.

In a high performance organization, you would have zero percent of the work group in the disengaged category, no more than 15 percent in the middle group and the balance, approximately 85 percent of the work group, engaged. Imagine what it would be like in your work setting, without spending one more nickel on personnel costs, if 85 percent were engaged and nobody worked to undermine you? Imagine an organization where nobody is working against management and most people work at the highest levels!

My job in taking an organization to a high performance level is to help the business owner or executive expand the engaged group of employees. Sometimes the disengaged can be converted through counseling to become a part of the engaged group, which is a logical and preferable choice because there has been an investment made in all employees. The costs in time and money associated with recruitment and hiring are significant and must be considered. Additionally, it isn't good to have a reputation of throwing away people as a first resort when encountering a problem.

More realistically, the best and most achievable outcome is to convert the disengaged to the middle group (neither engaged nor disengaged) and instill a disinclination to backslide. If they cannot be converted, my objective is to extricate them from the organization. This may sound cold, but in a business climate where you have to do more with less, all employees must be firing on all cylinders at all times.

After you build a high performance organization, the next objective is to keep it a high performance organization. My favorite personality theorist is Erik Erikson. He developed what he called the Epigenetic Chart of eight stages of personality development. The seventh stage is the place we spend most of our lifetime. Erikson titled this seventh stage "generativity vs. stagnation." He said we are either generating or we are stagnating. We are generating our families, meaning the next generation, our careers, and our personal and professional growth. Or, we are stagnating. There is, for Erikson, no middle ground. Once we have achieved the high performance status, we have to keep achieving. I completely agree and believe in this saying: "Good, better, best, never let it rest until your good is better and your better is best." Possibly annoying, but totally true. It's how you become an achiever.

Think about entropy, an engineering term meaning anything left alone will break down. If you don't replace the oil in your car, the oil in the engine will degrade, fail to do its job, and the engine will seize up. If you have a relationship with someone, and you don't invest yourself in the relationship, the relationship will fail. If you are trying to go up a down escalator, you will ultimately go down. Because there are so many factors working against becoming a success, you have to move fast or even run to get to the top of the "escalator." If you are standing still (stagnating), you will actually lose ground. Even if you are walking up on the down escalator, you are probably making no upward progress (stagnating). Only if you are moving fast or running will you get to the top (generativity). In a high performance organization, all parties from owner to vender to employees are running most, if not all, of the time.

Now back to the case. This was a high performance health care organization that hired Corinne as a mid-level technocrat. Although she wasn't a professional like a nurse, physical therapist, or social worker, she still had an important job as an intake worker certifying that the patient coming into the facility was qualified under the Medicare program. Once the certification was made, the paperwork for Medicare reimbursements was completed and submitted. The paperwork and the process had to be completed correctly or the government would make no payments to the facility providing the care. It was very detailed, important, and exacting work. Her annual salary was $36,000.

Corinne was about 45 years old and happened to be obese. After about 30 days on the job, those who were training Corinne decided that she was just not getting "it." After the sixth or seventh attempt to explain how the process for this and that was done and after fielding multiple requests for clarification of the same points, the orientation and training personnel determined that Corinne was too slow and not qualified to do the job. Being African-American and being obese had nothing to do with the fact that Corinne could not do her job. Remember, this was a high performance organization. People were moving fast, getting things done. In a different organization, there may have been more tolerance for a slow learner, but not here. When it became apparent that Corinne didn't get it and couldn't keep up, she became known as "Slow Fat Frita" behind her back. As cruel as this sounds, the reality is that it happens especially in a high performance setting where not only competence, but also speed is the expected norm.

The training and orientation lead worker, Susan, was a bit younger, perhaps 35 years old, and Caucasian. Remember, a lead worker is by definition an engaged person. Nobody should ever put a disengaged person in charge of training and orientating new people. Susan advised her boss that Corinne wasn't getting it and recommended he get let her go. Susan's boss, Michael, did not want to give up on Corinne. Time, money, and his credibility were tied up in recruiting and selecting her. Michael encouraged Susan to keep trying, but he was engaged in wishful thinking. Despite the interventions, Corinne was not able to do the job.

So, what did happen? Another month went by and Corinne fumbled and bumbled around the department. Her training mate, Susan, gave up on her and did the certifications herself. Engaged people don't complain; they just pick up the slack. Corinne went to Michael and complained, "They won't help me, don't like me, must be because I am Black." Oops — big problem. Now Michael has a potential race-based discrimination allegation on his hands.

An allegation usually "screams" to be investigated. It is neither a truth nor falsehood unless it is investigated and either substantiated or overturned. I was called in to deal with the allegation. This was a little different from the usual situation in that I was not being called into the organization to "get to the bottom" of the allegation but to make a determination if Corinne was discriminated against because she was African-American. I was called in extricate her and avoid a legal battle.

Michael knew that Susan was a highly engaged person with great credibility. She was not prejudiced against Corinne because of her race but rather because she was too slow and basically incompetent at the job. He now knew he had waited too long to say goodbye to Corinne. Had he acted when Susan first alerted him to the problem and had he acted upon the recommendations of the trainer, he could have evoked his rights to terminate without recourse under the premise of probation. Now, with this allegation, he really had a mess on his hands by his hands.

Remember that Corinne was a two-month employee in this organization who was still on probation. A probationary employee officially has no rights and can be terminated with or without cause *except* if there is discrimination. An employee of only one day has the right to a workplace free of discrimination says the Civil Rights Act of 1964. If an allegation of discrimination on the basis of race, age, or gender could be sustained, in this case by Corinne, there could be a big, big payday.

The real problem was that Corinne could not admit that she was too slow and/or simply not able to do this job. Rather than admit that she had failed, she chose to blame her trainer and brand her as a racist. My job was to get Corinne out of the organization without a big, expensive fight. Even if this is my job, I still must investigate the allegation as an independent person and make sure for myself that there is no race-based discrimination involved.

My first meeting with the organization was with Michael and his boss, the CEO, where I received my overview of the situation and my instructions. I had worked for this client before and understood the situation pretty well. The CEO established the organizational climate or culture as that of "high performance." It was clear that Michael needed to work on his interviewing skills, as well as trusting his trainer and acting on her recommendations.

The second meeting was with Corinne. After speaking with my client, I always speak next with the person making the allegation. In this case, I listened to Corinne's story allowing her to tell it without being interrupted. I never communicate any judgment at this meeting — I just listen. It is very important for the alleged victim to have his or her say and feel validated. While I cannot validate the substance of the story because I have only started the investigation, I can and should validate his or her worth as a person by listening attentively and showing respect. In this case, senior management had drawn its own conclusions about what happened. My job was not to rubber stamp them but to try and corroborate their findings. Remember, when I terminate Corinne, I am taking on legal liability. I had to make sure for myself that Corinne was not discriminated against because of her race.

Following the interview with Corinne was one with Susan in order to hear her side of the story. She told me that she had shown Corinne how to complete the certification and had kept specific and dated notes. Looking into the micro aspects of the situation, it was pretty clear that Susan was a superstar producer and that she did not "suffer fools" well. She could spot a producer when she worked with one, and Corinne was definitely not in this category. Susan knew that there was a lot to get accomplished in an eight-hour day, and if you were a "chatty Cathy" or too slow, you would never get the work done and consequently drag the team down. She had Corinne pegged. I asked Susan to explore the matter from several points of view and to be completely honest and candid with me about the prospect of prejudice due to race. She denied allowing race into the equation. Thanking her, I told her I'd get back to her if I needed to speak to her again. Susan was very credible, but I knew I would have to speak with her peers to be sure.

I then got Michael to provide an organizational chart identifying the names and titles of every one of his direct reports. Armed with this, I had names and titles of others who might corroborate or undermine Susan's statements. I spoke separately to four women, three Caucasian and one African-American who also had direct contact with Corinne. They all commented to me that she was slow. In response to a request for clarification of "slow," they talked about Corinne's physical movement as well as her comprehension of how the department and its processes worked. Their impression was that Corinne didn't get things done correctly, even after having them explained and demonstrated several times over several days. Two of the four commented about Corinne's proclivity to make chit-chat. They even thought that she tried to cover up her inability to understand things through excessive talking.

When asked if they liked Corinne personally, none of them said that they gotten that far with her. No one said that they didn't like her, which was a very interesting point. In a high performance organization, liking a person doesn't come into the picture until after the person's productivity is obvious or proven. People are hired into an organization to produce or accomplish things. Correct?

In reality, we all have to earn respect, but we shouldn't have to earn courtesy. Being treated with courtesy should be a given in a professional setting, but respect must be earned through one's productivity or performance. In a high performance organization, courtesy sometimes is shorted a bit because productivity is so highly prized and prioritized. Only after productivity is established does the interpersonal domain come into play. High performance organizations can be described as "high task" and "low relationship." Typical organizations strive to be "high task" and "high relationship." Government settings are usually "low task" settings. We have all heard the expression, "Close enough for government work."

I further asked these four employees, Susan's peers, what they thought of her. I asked, "Was she fair? Had she ever talked about Corinne? What did she say about Corinne?" I asked if Susan ever used racial terms to describe Corinne and if Susan had ever used terms to describe anyone in racial or ethnic terms before.

What I learned was that Susan was a top producer — a no-nonsense superstar. She knew everything necessary to operate the department and was a good trainer. She was not a racist and was known to be fair, but not tolerant of people who did not put 100 percent into their work. It turns out she was not considered a very sympathetic person — personable and with a sense of humor, but not sympathetic. One of her co-workers said to me that she was told (by Susan) "If you are looking for sympathy, it is in the dictionary, right there between sh*t and syphilis!" For Susan, work clearly was the priority. I could have interviewed other people outside the department to gain other insights into both of their reputations but decided against it as I did not wish to expose any of the parties to any further speculation nor did I want the rumor mill activated throughout the organization. I was confident that I had all the information I needed.

So now my investigation was complete, and I was convinced that the CEO and Michael's confidence in Susan was warranted. I was also confident that Corinne was not discriminated against because she was African-American. When I reported my findings to Michael and the CEO, neither was surprised and both, especially Michael, were relieved to have my corroboration and support.

So, what happened next in this pursuit to a solution that would avoid a race-based discrimination charge? My first question to Michael was "Are there any steps you need to take to cover the absence of Corinne after she is gone?" This is an important question in most cases because the person being extricated is usually producing or accomplishing something, and those contributions need to be delegated to someone else. There must be planning done to ensure a smooth transition. In this case, since Corinne was a trainee and others were already taking up the slack, no delegating of her duties was necessary.

Michael would need to lock down Corinne's remote computer access and hold a meeting with the others in the department to advise them that Corinne was gone. This would need to be done carefully because there were confidentialities to protect. Corinne had confidentiality rights, yet the staff needed to be told of the change. I coached Steve regarding what he should and should not say. If he violated her privacy rights, the costs to settle the case could rise dramatically. Embarrassing Corinne within the organization (even though she was leaving) must be avoided. An organization's values are on display with every decision and act. Everyone was watching to see how Corinne would be treated. An organization is judged by how it handles tough situations.

The choices that my client faced were two: We could go with termination and face her recourse, or we could negotiate with her and create a structured exit. The organization could merely terminate Corinne using employment-at-will statutes. Most states have laws that say that employees are employed at the "will of the employer," and if the employer wills to let them go, the employer can simply terminate them. This is a very weak defense for the employer to use because there are several protected classes of employees. Protected classes trumps employment-at-will in most cases. Using employment-at-will is like going into a gun battle with a small knife. The employer could also fall back on the fact that Corinne was on probation, which means that she had no rights to recourse. This too would be a weak argument because she had asserted race discrimination, which was a serious allegation.

There was legal recourse available to Corinne. As was mentioned above, she could file a charge with the EEOC or the state human rights commission or file a case in civil court. She could badmouth the organization in its marketplace. She also has two years (the usual the statute of limitations on this kind of case) in which to exercise her rights to legal recourse. If you were the CEO, would you like this matter hanging over your head for two years? I wouldn't.

Establishing a plan from the two alternatives and timetable for Corinne's extrication was next. I met with Michael and the CEO to work out what the organization was willing to pay or provide Corinne to get her out. The first thing to consider is what would this mess cost the organization if it did blow up and go to litigation or an administrative hearing with EEOC? There would be legal bills from defense lawyers and settlement bills that could be fines to the EEOC or state human rights commission as well as restitution to Corinne if she won the case. These things could add up to big dollars; it had the potential to be a $100,000 mess! Leaders of an organization usually have no idea of the storm they could be entering. They started to get the idea during this meeting with me.

My suggestion was for the organization to negotiate her exit strategy, which I would facilitate. What I suggested to the CEO and Michael was that we offer her a way out without resorting to litigation. I proposed that we offer her a deal. She could voluntarily resign and get something now, or she could be terminated now without compensation but possibly get something in the future through the recourses she had available to her. It was a small payday now with certainty and no fight or a big payday in the future with great uncertainty. Handled correctly, the former would be in Corinne's interest.

I needed to get my "marching orders" from my client. I suggested a severance package. There are three models for severance:

- Most generous — 30 days pay for each year of service
- Least generous — one week's pay for each year of service
- Most typical — two weeks pay for each year of service

Corinne had only been employed for two months so you might wonder what model made the most sense. I recommended that we offer her two month's pay. While this amount was slightly higher than the norm, this case had the potential for huge expenses if it went to court. Any time you go to court on a race-based discrimination charge, it's a battle of lawyers and a roll of the dice as to the outcome. Michael and the CEO really did not like having to offer her anything. Their question and the one everyone in this situation asks was, "You mean we have to pay her to leave?" The answer is actually yes and no. You are paying the employee to leave, but you are also paying him or her to waive rights to recourse. As distasteful as that notion is, it is cheaper than the cost of a legal fight. Sometimes there are considerations of providing access to health insurance continuation or other benefits. In this case, that did not come into play.

My clients did give me permission to offer the severance package of two months pay if necessary. Perhaps she would settle for less. I usually advise that we also offer a neutral reference and an agreement not to contest an application for state unemployment insurance. In this case, Corinne did not work at the job long enough to qualify for state unemployment insurance, but when applicable it is a good bargaining chip. Sometimes I suggest the employer offer to allow the exiting employee keep his or her laptop computer or cell phone. I did not suggest these in this case.

In terms of how this process would start, I suggested that Michael (since he was Corinne's supervisor) and I meet with her. I never expect my clients to have to do much since they have hired me to handle the situation for them. The first meeting in this phase was for me to establish my role and for the client organization to formally notify Corinne that I had been selected and authorized to address this matter going forward. Michael only had to speak if there was some material or factual clarification needed throughout the rest of the meeting. Otherwise, he just needed to sit there and stay quiet.

The next step was to convey that the organization had decided to terminate the employment relationship and that we were sorry that things did not work out as hoped. I pointed out that the employer organization has the right to take this step. I did not go over the reasons at this point because that would only serve to "rub it in" and start things off on an adversarial basis. I stated only that the position or job was ending and never allowed this meeting to become a debate or leave the door open that something she could say would change the situation. The decision to end the employment relationship was final, and all that remained was how that end would be formalized.

I proposed an alternative to being terminated that would allow Corinne to exit with the dignity associated with not being fired, with the ability to seek the next job without a termination record, and with some assistance from the current employer. After I gave Corinne a document that delineated an agreement that would allow her to exit under more favorable circumstances than termination, I told her to leave for the day to read it. I assured her that she was not fired at this point and that this full day would be paid. I wanted her to go home, read the document, consider its contents, and meet with me within the next two days to discuss it. I further assured her that I would clarify all aspects of the document and answer all her questions and concerns. She was also asked to leave her personal belongings which would be secured, protected, and given to her later.

After asking for her key to the facility, I walked her to her car and asked her not to do anything "provocative" or say or do anything that might harm her position with the organization. She should not call people at work until she has had a chance to talk and we have reached our agreement. I told her that we will not say anything to her workmates yet, that we intended to be professional and honor her rights to privacy and confidentiality, and asked her to do the same. After exchanging phone numbers, I told her that we would make contact tomorrow and arrange to meet at a coffee shop convenient to her home. This gave her time to think about the document and absorb its meaning. Trying to accomplish all of this at that point would be impossible as well as unfair to her. She needed time to adjust to what was happening. Once more, I assured her that she would be treated respectfully and professionally and that everything would work out.

At this point, I went back to Michael to go over what happened. Looking back over the meeting, I asked him if he thought I handled everything professionally and treated Corinne with dignity and respect. This is never the time to be flip or to use humor. It is a critical time and needs to be expertly handled. Not only were we in the liability hot zone, but the foundation for trust was being built between Corinne and me. She would not cooperate with me if she didn't trust or like me. It also provided an opportunity to help Michael be proactive as I reminded him that his choices had brought him here. Had he made other choices, the costs to remedy would be far lower.

Corinne and I met in her home at her insistence even though I usually don't like meeting in someone's home — its too personal. Coffee shops or restaurants are better because people "behave better" in a public setting. When we met, she was polite and apologized for the state of the house. She said she needed to clean and polish silver, and this was a good opportunity to get it done. I looked at the pictures of her kids and husband trying to find areas where we could relate, and we talked for about 30 minutes about her adult kids and their challenges. We were both parents of adult kids and had similar concerns, fears, and frustrations, which allowed for a communication that was neither condescending nor manipulative. There was no hurry, more like a conversation between friends. It turned out that I actually found her to be a thoroughly delightful and nice person, someone I would enjoy knowing.

Steering the conversation to business, I told her that I did not feel that Susan discriminated against her for race-based reasons. From my investigation, it was determined there was no discrimination, and I reminded her that the organization was an "all business" place, not wanting to using the term high performance with someone being extracted. It would give her the impression that she wasn't high performance, and my objective was not to educate her on what she could have done or change for next time, but rather to get her to the point of voluntary resignation. This would not happen if I offended her or appeared to preach at her.

I told Corinne that the organization did not take the time to get to know her as a person. I am very careful not to "throw my client under the bus" at any time, but it is acceptable to explain that the clients are so focused on productivity that they sometimes miss getting to know people which is what happened here. I stressed that the organization just wasn't that personable a setting, and she got caught up in a situation where the employer organization was just a bad match for her. It was something she could not have known when she hired on because the organization's interpersonal dynamics usually aren't discussed during an interview. I reassured her that being a bad match for the organization didn't make her a bad person or the organization a bad place. The organization did not know her well enough to realize what a great person she was; it wasn't their focus. My objective was to steer her away from taking this personally and being offended. There was little discussion about the agreement document during this first meeting. Instead, the conversation focused on answering her questions about the investigation and findings.

After 90 minutes, I called a halt to the meeting. There is a premise that I have always considered valuable: "The mind can only absorb what the butt can endure." We set a meeting for the next day as the more time I spent with her, the more trust and relationship I could build. It was made clear that our objective would be to go through the agreement.

The next day, after a brief, friendly conversation, I asked if she had read and was ready to review the document. She answered in the affirmative to both questions, and we were off to the races. I went paragraph by paragraph, stopping after each point to explain it and check for understanding. In the document, it clearly stated that this was a "hold harmless" agreement. This meant that Corinne agreed not to exercise any of her right to recourse with prejudice. I made it clear that by signing the document, she was waiving all her rights to take any legal or public action against the organization permanently, and that this agreement was enforceable in a court of law. The agreement went both ways with the organization agreeing not to say anything bad about her or take any action against her. The agreement put the matters permanently in both participants' rear view mirrors, which was the priority from my client's point-of-view.

Imbedded in the document was the severance package but not the full eight weeks agreed upon by the organization. I held some back so that I could be "argued up" by Corinne. This is an important point in the negotiation; the person being extricated needs to feel like he or she got "the better" of the company. In reality, I rarely offer what my client authorizes me to pay so I can then "offer it up" later. I draw the process out so that I do not appear to be the one approving the counter offer, indicating that I will speak with the organization and get their reaction. While this slows the process down, it is an advantage in most instances. It shouldn't be too quick or easy and must appear that I am dragging the extra money or whatever the person wants out of the former employer. This process earned me more credibility with Corinne that I was not only helping her but getting her a better deal. She felt like she had a victory. After each meeting, I called back to Michael or the CEO and provided a progress report and my opinion on the negotiation.

In the end, Corinne accepted the two months pay and signed the document, thereby closing the case. I guessed that she accepted this amount because she had only been an employee for two months. Her reasoning was that by accepting the job offered by the employer, she took herself out of the market and bypassed the other opportunities for which she was in contention. Maybe true, maybe not. By accepting the two months additional pay, it was like she was getting double: two months of work and two more months to cover her while she looked for a new job seemed symmetrical and logical.

For my client organization, it was a small price to pay (about $6,000) for avoiding a race-based discrimination claim, and for Corinne it was vindication. It did not require her to face a fight that she may or may not have won. Sure, she might have won a big payday possibly two or three years down the road, but that would have meant two or three years of meetings, legal proceedings, and a significant amount of time dealing with the unpleasant past. Six grand now without a fight and without a potential loss in the case was attractive and clearly in her interest.

By the way, I had to take my check to the bank personally — it was too little to go by itself! Joking aside, my fee and the settlement to Corinne was a very small fraction of the amount that could have been spent on a legal battle.

Management Lessons

1. The manager's goal should be to establish a "high performance" organization. This means having a very large percentage (over 70%) of your direct reports "engaged" and none "disengaged." Some might be in a third category of neither engaged nor disengaged, but you cannot afford for employees to be disengaged and working against you. If they are in this category and cannot be converted to another category, they should be extricated.

2. There are legal differences regarding the rights of employees on probation vs. their rights after they complete probation. A probationary employee can be terminated with or without cause, and they have no legal rights to due process. Once probation has ended, the employee has the right to at least an oral warning and a written warning prior to termination. Standard probationary periods are usually 90 days. I recommend that probation be set at 180 days for hourly employees and 1 year for supervisors. Ninety days is just not enough time to assess the "fit" between the employee and the organization. A bad fit will portend bad things, and a bad hire is far worse than no hire. The longer the probationary period, the more time management has to evaluate and judge the employee's fit. If a bad fit is judged to exist, management can sever the relationship without going through due process. If the employee has passed through his or her probation, then management is obligated to go through the oral and written warning stages in order to terminate.

3. Employees have rights relating to their confidentiality, and employers must protect these rights. It is inappropriate and violates the employee's rights to confidentiality to discuss disciplinary information or the reason someone was terminated with other employees. It is necessary to advise employees that other employees have been terminated or leave voluntarily; however, the reasons for the exit are confidential. If asked for the reasons for the exit, supervisors should be instructed to say, "That information is confidential and not something that I can discuss." A good follow -up comment could be, "You wouldn't want me to discuss the reasons for your termination with others if the situation were reversed, am I right?"

4. If termination is selected, there are several steps that management should consider. Advise the terminated employee that the decision has been made – that it is not a debate. While they cannot argue or discuss getting their job back, they can protect their "good will" with the company. If an employee were to create a "scene," there is the possibility that he or she could damage a future reference from that employer. In most cases, do not rehash the reasons for the decision to terminate. You have already talked to this person, perhaps on multiple occasions, about their shortcomings. This is a time to sever the relationship. Protect their self-esteem and terminate the job the employee did, not the person. There is a big difference between "There was a bad outcome to your efforts." vs. "You failed." or "You screwed it up."

5. Avoid the "perp walk" out of the facility. If possible, allow the terminated employee to leave the building and then return after hours, under escort, to obtain his or her personal items. Preserve the exiting employee's dignity by agreeing to meet after hours to help retrieve personal belongings.

Chapter 3

Nepotism and Organizational Integrity: The Case of the Office Sniper and Agitator

This case began with the death of the beloved mother-in-law of Jackie, a billing expert in a large medical billing company. Jackie was no angel, but she was a superstar. She managed a "book of business" that had been seriously problematic in the past due to mismanagement. The person taking care of this particular group of accounts had created big problems; Jackie came in, straightened everything out, and made her bosses very happy. She was not perfect but a superstar none-the-less.

Jackie, 32 and African-American, worked in a company that did the Medicare billing for 100 or so practices throughout the country and employed a large number of mostly tech-savvy young women. These employees did not have college degrees and were typically paid around $18.00 per hour, which was good money for their high school level of education. The work was very exacting and required a highly detailed person to do it well. Unfortunately, the work was very repetitive and once the employees "got" the process, it didn't occupy their whole attention. For many it was not very stimulating, so for some employees a bit of office drama was required to keep things interesting. This was definitely true for one employee, a biller named Mary. Before I introduce Mary and the drama she caused, let me give you the background.

Again, Jackie was truly amazing at her job. She knew it and so did her bosses and everyone else in the office. One of Jackie's peers was a 63-year-old Caucasian woman, Beth, who worked in a nearby cubicle. For some reason, on an occasion about six months before the passing of Jackie's mother-in-law, there was an incident between Jackie and Beth. Jackie had a very public yelling fit directed at Beth. In the course of this yelling fit, she told Beth that she was too old to do her job and should be fired. Beth, who had two sons who happened to be lawyers, reported the incident to senior management and alleged that she had been "assaulted" by Jackie. She wanted Jackie fired from her job and one of her sons to file assault charges in a criminal case.

I was called in, conducted an investigation, and determined that there had been no assault. I tried to help Beth understand that she had been insulted or offended, but not assaulted after which she said no criminal charges would be filed. In response to whether she was too old to do her job, she replied "no," and I informed her that her bosses felt the same way. Jackie's opinion was not shared by anyone of importance, and Beth was advised to "let it go." Despite the fact that even her sons felt she had overreacted, she couldn't. Ultimately, Jackie got a reprimand, and Beth harbored a grudge of deep-seated resentment.

Now, fast-forward about six months to when Jackie's mother-in-law passed away. She had been very close to her mother-in-law and had made arrangements for a "celebration of her life" party in her own home, rather than a traditional wake or funeral. This arrangement had been planned previously with the then seriously ill mother-in-law's approval. Evidently, nobody in the family wanted a sad event, but rather a joyous celebration of her life. Fine. The problem was that Jackie brought her personal life into the office. For some reason, she had asked for, and received permission to, issue a company-wide invitation. It seemed to me that this event should have been for family and friends, not business associates, but Jackie invited everyone from the office to attend. Four "friends" from work showed up, two with their kids, and they were in attendance for several hours. The celebration of the mother-in-law's life seemed to come off just fine as everyone was joyful; there were no tears of sadness. As far as Jackie knew, everyone went home satisfied with the celebration. Wrong!

One of the attendees was Mary. She attended with her fiancé who happened to be the "loser" son of one of the company owners. I say loser son because he had a drug problem and was so unreliable he had already been fired from his parents' company. Every employee knew that the son, about 25 years old, was a derelict, and they were glad to see him gone. Mary was attractive, 22, and saw the son as a good catch. He was the only son of the owners (husband and wife owned 51% of the company) who were worth millions. Loser son could conceivably straighten up in the future, and in the meantime, gave Mary some bulletproofing. She was a charmer who always had an excuse or an alibi for the havoc that seemed to occur in her wake. Loser son considered Mary a good catch because of her looks.

Now, you should know that Mary had screwed up no less than five times in the past year alone and while she had been written up, she hadn't been fired. Any other employee would have been fired after the second or third incident. Everyone, including Mary, knew this. The 49% owner, Brad (the COO), operated the company and was frustrated with Mary's protection by the wife of the other owner. Mary was not a friend of Jackie's but probably attended the "celebration of life" party in Jackie's home simply because she was invited. That next Monday, Mary, while gossiping at work, explained to her friends that the event was a totally inappropriate way to mourn a person's death and that, by the way, there might have been some illegal drug use going on during the party. Mary followed these statements with the racial slur that conducting a celebration of life event instead of a traditional wake must be some "African or African-American thing."

When Jackie heard from her friends what Mary had been saying, she just caught on fire. She went straight to Brad and filed a serious complaint. He understood how personally Jackie was taking these accusations. After all, she had just buried her mother-in-law and then heard through the grapevine that the office troublemaker had made a racist assertion that the way she chose to recognize and celebrate the life of her mother-in-law was inappropriate. Added to that was the assertion (allegation) that there may have been drugs present. Brad could easily see why Jackie was freaked. His problem was that the incident took place away from the work site, and the resulting allegations had nothing to do with work. However, they had spilled over into the workplace and turned into a stinking mess with the additional prospect for violence and race-based considerations factored in the mix.

Brad advised Jackie that since the incident did not occur at work, there was nothing that he could do and advocated handling the matter outside of work. He deeply regretted allowing Jackie to invite people from work to attend the celebration of life event. Jackie, well known for her temper, was still seething but accepted his judgment. She allowed a few days to pass and attempted to put the matter behind her until she saw Mary smirk and act as if she had "won." Meanwhile, the office gossip mill was in full swing. On Jackie's side, some urged her not to allow Mary to get away with it while others urged her to be very careful. Those who supported Mary seemed to be loving the office drama. Meanwhile, Brad and the office supervisors were noticing a precipitous lack of productivity.

At the end of her shift and technically off-duty, Jackie approached Mary and ordered her to follow her outside of the building because "they needed to talk." After a brief conversation outside of the building, Mary went to Brad, told him that Jackie had just threatened her with bodily harm and that she was fearful for her safety. Brad now had a mess that was escalating. And, he was over his head.

Called in to consult, I met with Brad, along with the office supervisors, and they confirmed that Mary was a real pain and had been from the day she started dating the owners' son. The office supervisors wanted Mary terminated, but Brad knew that termination could result only if certain stars aligned properly because the majority owner's wife seemed to always believe Mary's version of every story. I was authorized to conduct a thorough examination of the allegations made by Jackie against Mary, as well as Mary's allegation that Jackie threatened her.

My first meeting was with Jackie. We knew each other because of the incident six months earlier when she asserted that Beth was too old to work at the company. Jackie remembered me and assured me that this incident was very different. We focused on the current set of circumstances. She reiterated the facts as she saw them and stated that she did not threaten Mary. She only wanted to talk to her to clear the air and that was all that happened. Jackie gave me the names of several of her coworkers who could verify that she behaved professionally and would not threaten Mary. She told me how aggravated she was to learn of Mary's comments regarding the celebration of her mother-in-law's passing. In addition, she assured me that there were no drugs present at the party and that I could check with the other three employees who were in attendance.

I took their names and further questioned Jackie about the conversation with Mary. Jackie had a pretty good story. Apparently, she told Mary that she did not appreciate her gossiping and that she had filed a formal complaint with management. That was all, over in less than two minutes. I thanked her, advised her not to take any action or to do anything that could be considered provocative relative to Mary and told her that I would get to the bottom of things. She agreed to put her feelings on hold and let me do my job.

Next I met with Mary who turned out to be oh so smooth. We started with the allegation that Jackie threatened her with bodily harm. I asked her to take me through the confrontation step-by-step, detail-by-detail. Mary told me Jackie came up to her and ordered her to come outside to talk. When they got outside the building, she told me she was threatened when Jackie told her that she knew where she lived. Mary told me that Jackie said that she was going to get her for what she did. She was teary and assured me that she had done nothing to deserve being threatened. I asked her what she did when Jackie threatened her. She said she turned around without saying anything and ran back into the office. The exchange took less than a few minutes.

I moved on to the allegations about Mary's statements and asked her if she had told her friends anything about the party when she returned to work the following Monday. Mary told me that she told her friends that the party was nice but nothing about it being inappropriate or making any reference to African or African-American culture. I asked her whom she said this to, and she supplied their names. I further questioned her about the presence of drugs at the party. Mary told me that she thought she smelled pot while at the party but didn't see anybody smoking it. She told me that she did not mention anything to anybody about the presence of drugs at the party.

Returning to the subject of the threat of bodily harm, I asked Mary to relate what she did upon her return from the encounter. She told me that it took some time to settle down and decide what to do. Then she reported the incident to Brad and sought his help and protection. Mary told me that the confrontation had occurred at the end of Jackie's shift but that her shift had another hour. At the end of her shift, she asked Brad if he would walk her to her car because she was afraid that Jackie might be waiting for her in the underground parking lot. She claimed that he refused her request, and she was forced to walk to her car alone. She asked me if the situation constituted a workplace problem and then provided me with several names of employees who could verify that Jackie was a bully — someone to be fearful of and careful around.

I thanked Mary for her input and advised her that I would talk to the other employees. Similar to Jackie, I suggested that she focus on her job, stay away from Jackie, and allow me to conduct my investigation, to let the facts speak for themselves. Then Mary asked me about getting a restraining order and any possible impact that action could have on her job to which I responded that I was not sure and could not advise her.

This was the point where Beth entered the situation. I had interviewed all of the people whom Jackie and Mary had suggested. Each one provided insights that supported claims that the other person was bad or a problem. Then, something very interesting happened. Beth asked to see me because she had information relating to the confrontation that Jackie had precipitated with Mary. She told me that she had been at the copy machine next to the door that led out of the building and had heard Jackie order

Mary to follow her through that door. She recognized the tone in Jackie's voice and feared for Mary's safety because she knew how dangerous Jackie could be. She further reported that she actually heard some of what Jackie said as the door had closed rather slowly. Beth reminded me that she had once been assaulted by Jackie and knew what Jackie was capable of doing.

Continuing, she told me that she feared so much for Mary's safety, she called 911 on her cell phone and told the operator what was happening. The operator asked if there was a supervisor or someone else present who could be notified and intercede immediately. Beth acknowledged that there were supervisors present but that the situation was potentially so dangerous police might be needed. As the operator was confirming if it was a call for police, Mary came back through the door and returned to her workstation. Jackie did not return so the situation seemed to be less critical and no police were needed. The operator signed off, and Beth went back to her copy work.

Naturally, I had to find out why Beth felt it necessary to call 911 when the supervisor and Brad were on-site and available to assist at a moment's notice. Did she have any idea about the ramifications of bringing the police into the situation? She told me that she didn't know why she didn't call someone who was there and did not think about any ramifications or consequences. She just repeated that Jackie was capable of violence and that she feared for Mary's safety.

When I asked Beth what she knew about Mary, she acknowledged that they weren't friends but that Mary seemed like a hard worker and a good person. In response to my question regarding Mary's reputation for spreading rumors or gossip, she admitted that there had been one incident when Mary overheard something that Beth had said and mischaracterized it as she gossiped with her friends. She assured me that the incident was a minor one, and she had let the matter drop. Beth would not or could not tell me why she had been able to let her own problem with Mary drop, but not the one concerning Jackie.

It seemed obvious to me that Beth's incident with Jackie was still overtly causing her concern, which made me wonder if it wasn't another case of overreacting. Beth asserted that she did not overreact then or now and was just telling me what happened. Once again, she expressed her concern for Mary's safety.

After each day in my investigation, I provided Brad with an interim report of my salient findings. When informed of Mary's claim that he would not walk her to the underground parking lot, he was stunned. This revelation was very significant. Mary had to know that I would confront Brad in an attempt to confirm the statement. It is one thing to tell lies and spread rumors about one's coworkers. It is clearly another thing to make accusations against the COO. This incident served to prove that Mary was a liar and a troublemaker. For her to be able to sustain her position in the face of this situation would only serve to make her bolder then ever. Wow.

My examination of the allegations now complete, I was ready to draft my report. My job was to advise management regarding my findings, provide appropriate recommendations, and place my client in the most defendable position to minimize or avoid any potential for wrongful discharge blow-back. What were the alternatives or the remedies in the situation? One choice could be to terminate Mary. She had a long history of gossiping and troublemaking throughout the organization, and her behavior in this case was certainly reprehensible. Another choice could have been to terminate Jackie. Her behavior and choices were inappropriate and unprofessional, and this incident was the second strike against her considering the incident with Beth. Taking one step back, either or both could simply be reprimanded with the incidences written up and placed in their files. I had to consider the recourse potential for either party if termination were to result from the incident.

I reported to Brad that I thought it was completely within character and plausible that Mary made the derogatory statements about the party and the prospect that illegal drugs were present. I also thought that it was within character and completely plausible that Jackie threatened Mary's safety. I advised him that the whole situation was serious as there was significant liability if the organization mishandled any aspect of the situation or its participants. Jackie would be within her rights to bring a race-based discrimination claim or charge against the organization if the organization took precipitous action (the legal term for termination) against her. I thought that if Mary were terminated, there would be a very small potential for her to file any action against the organization because of her relationship with the owners' son.

There was no credible evidence to substantiate the allegation that Jackie threatened Mary's safety. The conversation took place in a private setting between the two participants. Insights shared by Beth were so tainted by her resentment toward Jackie that they were not credible. I also acknowledged that Jackie was capable of threatening Mary. It was within the realm of understanding that she would be angry and even take action as a result of Mary's rumor-mongering behavior. Not that it was right, but that it was understandable.

Ultimately, I recommended that Mary be terminated and that Jackie be reprimanded. Mary would only become more emboldened by sustaining her position. I warned Brad that she was only a novice now, but given her impending marriage into the family business and several more years of experience successfully manipulating people and situations, she would become formidable. People like Mary file lawsuits, take advantage of laws and rules and leave a great deal of wreckage as they move through life. It may have sounded harsh, but I saw no redeeming characteristics in her. Brad then told me that Mary's mother had also survived on her looks alone and was someone who sought to take advantage of opportunities to file lawsuits. He was even aware of a judgment that had been won. Mary was just following in her mother's footsteps.

I recommended that Jackie only be reprimanded because there was no direct credible proof that she threatened her co-worker. If Jackie were terminated, she could easily make the case that the company showed favoritism toward Mary and discriminated against Jackie. There was plenty of evidence to show that the company was too lenient with Mary because of her fiancé's connections. Jackie was an attractive and very articulate woman. She would present herself as the top producer that she was. It would be very unlikely that Mary would take any action against the company if she were terminated. A place would probably be found for her somewhere else in her fiancé's family holdings or enterprises.

If Jackie were terminated, this would have a very chilling effect on the morale of the employees, African-American and otherwise, within the company. Jackie's termination would unleash Mary's power within the organization. The effect of all this drama would be so distracting, in my opinion, that overall productivity would take a nosedive.

I also had some thoughts and recommendations regarding the matter of Beth calling 911 in an attempt to summon the police. Beth was problematic within the organization. Her judgment was so impaired that she, through the choice of calling 911, could have done significant damage. Imagine the consequences of calling the police into an office setting. Usually, when the police come into a situation like this, someone gets arrested. At the very least someone, in this case probably Jackie, could have become so embarrassed and humiliated that any number of possibilities could be imagined. It was not outside the realm of possibility that such a situation could have driven Jackie to violence sometime in the near future. Imagine the impact on the office productivity had a police presence occurred. Imagine the capital that Mary could have achieved through police intercession in the situation. Beth considered none of these matters or possibilities. She overreacted and could have started a chain of events from which the organization might not have survived. I recommended that Beth be reprimanded and warned that she was to notify her supervisor or an owner if she had any concerns regarding any matter that related to work. She needed to understand that management considered her judgment so impaired that any future missteps would result in her immediate termination.

I attempted to help Brad understand how serious the situation was at this point and that it could have been even worse. If he could not get his partner to support him in taking the recommended actions, I did not see how he could continue to operate the company. In my opinion, Mary would become uncontrollable once she married into the family business, and Jackie would have an easily winnable legal course of action if she were mishandled. Beth was so impaired in her judgment that she couldn't be trusted to recognize, understand, and respond appropriately to almost any impingement in her environment.

In the end, Brad was unable to convince his partners that my recommendations should be implemented and they gave Mary one more chance. He assured me that she would mess up again and when she did, it wouldn't take him long to fire her. Then Brad told me that his partners did not appreciate my suggestions or recommendations even though he knew that they were correct and accurate. Assuring me that he would rely upon me and call me in the near future, I got paid and was dismissed.

Management Lessons

1. A business organization's values are on display in every decision the organization makes. The leaders in any organization establish and control the organizational climate. Employees are watching these decisions very closely and are vicariously experiencing every decision. How does the organization deal with misbehaviors? How does the organization deal with people who are basically screw-ups? Does the organization show favoritism to some and no mercy to others? When the leaders or owners of a business organization are themselves the problem, there is very little hope for good morale or high performance to exist. People are too smart and too observant to be conned. You cannot talk your way out of what you are behaving your way into.

2. Nepotism is favoritism granted to relatives without regard to merit of performance. The hiring of relatives of existing employees is fairly commonplace. It has its upsides and downsides. The main upside is familiarity —family members know one another, and therefore no time is needed to establish relationships and trust. The downsides, however, could be many. There is often baggage inherent in family relationships, and this baggage will inevitably be brought into the workplace. It is very hard for employees

who are also relatives to perform their work duties objectively. If the employer has problems with one family member, there is a high likelihood that those problems will spill over and affect the relationship the employer has with other family members who are also employees.

3. At the heart of the conflict in this case was the fact that the incident occurred outside of the workplace. Management was so confounded by this fact that it failed to react properly. Management cannot expect employees to deposit their emotions and their feelings in a holding bin by the front door and then retrieve them on the way out at the end of their shifts. We are all emotional, social, and sexual beings, and we carry our emotions and our worries into the workplace and everywhere else we go. It is a rare person who can segregate or wall off his or her personal life at work. Management needs to recognize that the stress of each employee's life will generally get factored into the workplace one way or another and must deal with the problems this can cause. In this case, management should have recognized the depth of the feelings about the mother-in-law that was exposed by the office troublemaker.

Chapter 4

Poor Leadership and Vendettas: The Police Chief Doesn't Like the Lieutenant

Originally, this was a case a year earlier that had the police chief accusing one of his deputies, the grandson of the town's mayor, of sexual harassment. The evidence was spotty but to avoid the fight and to expunge his work record, the grandson resigned, moved to another town, and joined their police department. The mayor did not believe his grandson committed any sexual harassment but chose not to intercede. He kept the incident in the back of his mind, the grandson obtained a new position, and life went on. The mayor, however, smelled a rat.

Fast-forward about 18 months. There was an allegation within the department by one of the female dispatchers, Alena, that a lieutenant, Sam, attempted to sexually assault her when she was on a "ride along" with him on a hot August Saturday night. A little background might be helpful. The dispatchers in most police departments are encouraged to "ride along" with officers from time to time so that they can gain an appreciation for what goes on during the police officer's shift in the field. This is what happened on that August evening. Alena was scheduled for the midnight to 8 AM shift and had elected to ride along with Sam prior to its beginning.

The allegation was that while they were driving, Sam turned off the air conditioner, turned on the heater, and after a while asked Alena if she was hot. She said yes, and Sam told her to take off her blouse. She said no, and he then drove to the cemetery and parked the car. The second allegation was that Sam moved across the console and got on top of her in an attempt to rape her. She somehow escaped his clutches and exited the car. Sam supposedly came to his senses, apologized, and convinced her to return to the car. He then drove her to the station to begin her shift.

Alena notified the chief who promptly suspended Sam and began to negotiate with him. The deal was that Sam would quit his job and move out of town in return for no charges filed. Instead, Sam went to the mayor, the police chief's boss, argued that he was set up, and proclaimed his innocence. The mayor, recalling what had happened to his grandson just 18 months earlier, smelled the same rat.

I received a call from the mayor with a request that I investigate the situation. An allegation of attempted sexual battery was a criminal matter, and I advised the mayor that my work was primarily civil. I suggested he contact the state police to conduct a criminal investigation. The mayor told me that he did not trust cops investigating cops. He did not think that there was an attempted rape, so therefore there was no criminal matter to investigate. He advised me that he wanted a civil investigation of a sexual harassment allegation. I reiterated that there was more here than a sexual harassment allegation and tried my best to dodge the assignment, but the mayor was adamant. He told me to come to his town and interview Sam. If I still felt that the assignment was inappropriate, then and only then would he accept my withdrawal from the case. Such persistence and adamancy was compelling.

I agreed and cleared my calendar for the trip. First, I met with the mayor and got the background on the incident, as well as learned about the experience the mayor's grandson had had with the chief. Under normal circumstances, my next interview would be with the person making the allegations. However, since this was the second time a sexual harassment situation had come up with this chief, I met with Sam to gather his story first. He told me that he was 40 years old and had been in law enforcement for 16 years. The chief and the captain hired him two years ago, and while he didn't get along that well with them, he did his job as the number three person in the department. Sam told me he had been married to "the best girl in the world" for 19 years and that he would never do anything to jeopardize his relationship with his wife. He wept as he showed me pictures. He said that he had never had this type of complaint against him or this kind of problem in his work setting. Since this allegation had occurred, he couldn't sleep and was urinating blood. The stress was so great, he was suffering physical ramifications from it. He begged for my help in clearing him and swore on his life that he was completely innocent. I decided that I would take this case and told Sam that I would let the mayor know that I would look into the allegations.

My first stop was a "courtesy call" to the chief of police. The chief made it clear to me that he didn't need my help but that he would cooperate with my investigation on orders from the mayor. I thought this was interesting considering what the mayor had told me about the chief and the incident with the mayor's grandson. I had dealt with many chiefs of police on past cases and generally found them to be "hard cases." Not bad people, just people who carry guns and are used to running roughshod over the law. They are the law in a paramilitary setting where the chain of command and the "blue wall of silence" always prevail. I could see why the mayor didn't really like this guy, but there wasn't enough here for me to distrust him yet.

The next meeting was with Alena and held away from the station house. Before I even opened my mouth to ask the first question or to invite Alena to recount the incidences of that night, I could not help but notice how phenomenally beautiful this woman was. She was a 15 on a 10-point scale, seemed intelligent. and was appropriately dressed and decorous in her manner. I found out that she was divorced with a 14-year-old who lived with her.

I asked Alena to take me through the events during the "ride along." She told me she entered the squad car at about 9 o'clock that evening, and they spent about 90 minutes or so cruising the streets, answering routine calls, and working two traffic stops. About 10:30, perhaps 10:45, the conversation turned a bit personal. She said that Sam told her how beautiful she was and how nicely she always dressed and acted. Alena told me she accepted the compliment and felt no concern at the time. Then she noticed that Sam was driving to a remote part of the city, had turned off the air conditioner, and turned on the heater. She thought this was strange because it was August, and the temperature was in the low 90s. After a while, she said that Sam asked her if she was hot and when she said yes, he told her to take off her blouse. She told me her response was one of embarrassment, and she tried to roll down the window but couldn't because Sam had the windows locked from his control panel. So, she just turned away and looked out the window, not knowing what else to do.

After that, Alena said Sam turned the air conditioner back on and started driving again as if nothing had happened. They sat in silence for about 10 minutes, and she noticed that they were turning into the cemetery. He drove to the back end, parked the car, and notified dispatch that he was taking a break and would be off the radio. She said Sam then came across the console and was on top of her, groping her and reaching into her pants. She fought and protested, but he ignored her. She was able to get him off of her and get out of the car before he raped her. He apologized and told her that he would take her back to work. She got back into the car, and they drove in silence back to the station where they exited the car still not speaking.

It is my practice to get interviews started by having the people I'm interviewing tell their full story. I try not to interrupt and I take detailed notes so that I can go back to ask clarifying questions and get additional details. Not interrupting shows respect and allows them to have their full say. I generally begin the interview advising the person I'm interviewing that everything he or she says will be held as confidentially as possible. In addition, I try to apologize for the indelicate nature of the situation and my questions, telling the person I'm interviewing that I need to understand as clearly as possible and that's the reason for my probing questions. The interview is kept on as professional a level as possible at all times. Alena's interview would require this kind of discretion.

In the interview, she recounted all of the events of the evening and left me with about a million questions. I took her back to the point where Sam allegedly turned off the air conditioner and turned on the heater. Were the windows were still rolled up? Answer yes. What setting was the blower on, low, medium, or high? She said she didn't know. Was the radio playing? She said yes. How long did the heater stay on before he asked her if she was hot? She told me over six minutes. Curious, I asked her how she knew it was about or over six minutes. She indicated that two songs played on the radio during that time, and the first one was Huey Lewis and the News singing "Happy to be Stuck with You." Alena even told me the name and call numbers of the radio station. I asked her to be as sure about this as possible. She assured me that the heater was on for the full time, and two songs were played. I made a note to confirm this fact by calling the radio station and asking the engineer to tell the exact time and the name of the song that followed the Huey Lewis and the News song.

In response to how she felt about being asked to take off her blouse, Alena told me that she knew it was inappropriate. She knew that Sam was a married man — pretty cute she said, but still a married man. While she felt he was a bit offensive at the start, she got "come-ons" from men all the time. I then asked her about the time in the cemetery. Was she concerned when he notified the dispatcher that he was going on break and off radio? Alena indicated that it happened so quickly, she almost didn't notice. Continuing to describe what happened next, she said he took off his seatbelt, came across the console and was on top of her in no time at all. She was pinned to the seat but tried to push him off and keep him from unsnapping her jeans. Then she told me it was too uncomfortable to keep talking about and asked if could we change the subject.

To go a slightly different direction, I asked her if she liked Sam as a person. She said yes he was nice enough and that the officers liked him well enough. Was there anything in his behavior or in his speech toward her that might have given her any hint that this was coming? She replied no, that he was professional, and his actions caught her completely off guard.

The next question was related to her escape at the cemetery and how she was able to get out of the car. Apparently, she got her seatbelt off, the door open and was then able to get out, moving away and behind one of the headstones. By this time, Sam was also out of the car and apologizing for what happened. He said he was sorry several times and asked her to please get back in the car; he wouldn't do anything but drive her back to the station. She said that she agreed to do so because she was stuck out at the edge of town and didn't want to walk back at night by herself. Alena added that they rode back to the station without speaking and as if nothing had happened.

Alena started her shift without making any comments to the dispatcher who was going off duty and notified the chief in the morning. She told me that the chief said he would take care of things. I asked her if the chief asked her if she wanted to press charges for attempted sexual battery, and she said no. The chief just told her that he would take care of everything, and that was that.

I thanked Alena and told her I would get back to her with further questions. The whole story was so appalling I hardly knew where to start. I had already spoken with Sam but felt it was important to follow my procedure so I made a second appointment. Since he was on administrative suspension, he had all the time I needed. I asked Sam to put on his uniform and vest exactly as he was wearing it that night two weeks before, as well as wear his utility gun belt exactly as he was wearing it on the night of the incident. We were going to replay the events of the allegations as stated by Alena. The only difference was that we were going to attempt to recreate the circumstances during the day, rather than at night. I asked Sam to invite his wife to participate and play the role of Alena for the re-creation and she agreed. We got into his assigned squad car and began driving. Sam and his wife occupied the front seat with me in the back. The temperature was in the upper 90's and pretty close to the nighttime temperature of the incident.

Sam turned off the air conditioner (the windows were already rolled up) and turned on the heater with the blower on low. I started my stopwatch and began to monitor the passage of time. After 60 seconds, it became uncomfortable. At 120 seconds, we began to sweat. At three minutes, I was covered with sweat and very uncomfortable. By the time we hit four minutes, it was so unbearable that we stopped the experiment, bailed out of the car, and then cranked up the air conditioning when we got back in. Sam looked like he was going to pass out as he was dressed in full uniform, Kevlar vest, and full utility belt. His wife was, like myself, covered with sweat and red-faced. It took several minutes with the air conditioner blower on high to recover from the incident. Clearly, there was no possible way the situation Alena described could have lasted six minutes.

We then drove to the cemetery at the edge of town and parked toward the back. The squad car had bucket seats separated by a 12-inch console that had three radios installed vertically between them. Again looking at my stopwatch, I instructed Sam to go across the console and attempt to simulate an attack on his wife sitting in the other seat. Both Sam and his wife were wearing their seatbelts, and by the time Sam unbuckled his seatbelt, raised the steering wheel to its most elevated position and began to attempt to move over the console, the person in the passenger seat would have had plenty of notice that something unusual was happening. He then attempted to get his large frame, with full utility belt attached, pivoted in an attempt to go over the radios installed in the console. There was no way that this man could get his big body over the console and around the steering column, let alone with the utility belt attached to his waist. It was impossible! The passenger would have had, or could have had, plenty of time to get her seatbelt off and out of the car if she needed to escape. Alena's story (the allegation) could not be substantiated. In fact, it had to be a lie.

Even though the three of us were convinced, I still had some facts and loose ends to tie up. I spoke with the engineer at the radio station only to discover that the song, "Happy to be Stuck with You" had not even been played on the night in question. The local office of the national weather bureau confirmed the temperature recorded for that night at that time.

I also interviewed seven police officers and two administrative personnel under Sam's command. They confirmed that he was an "all business" kind of supervisor and indicated that he was fair, knowledgeable, and firm, even though not particularly likable. All agreed that he brought professionalism to the department. When I asked them about the captain and the chief, their comments became muted and sparse. No one spoke badly about either, but I got the impression that their lack of comment was more out of fear than respect. What I did learn was that the chief and his captain were very close, spending most of their time together at the station as well as away from it. The officers on staff said Sam provided the real police leadership in the department.

My next meeting was with the mayor to report my findings. I shared the results of the simulation and formally advised him that the allegations against Sam could not be substantiated. They were undoubtedly lies. The mayor stopped me, placed a call to Sam, and told him to come to his office to hear the results of my report. I protested and suggested that it was premature to advise Sam prior to the report being formally presented. Brushing off my protest, the mayor insisted that Sam needed to be formally vindicated without delay. Sam's wife accompanied him. Wow! Before the mayor could really digest and discuss my findings, he had speed dialed Sam who had come immediately, lights on, siren blaring, and wife in tow. After I repeated my report, it was clear they were visibly relieved, and they wanted to know what the mayor and I were going to do about the situation. This is what I had feared as I was unprepared to provide anything but my speculation. The mayor, being the consummate politician, told them to go home, celebrate, and let him work it out. I reminded Sam that he had won the battle, but the war was still on. He needed to be patient, let future events unfold, and do nothing that might be considered provocative or harm his position.

When we were alone again, I advised the mayor that my job was over to which he responded, "Oh no, it's not. Now your job is to get to the bottom of why this happened." I sensed that what was going on was far deeper and more personal than what had appeared on the surface. The chief was not satisfied with just terminating Sam. Why was he attempting to "ash can" Sam's entire career? No individual with this kind of allegation on his record would ever be employable in law enforcement again. Despite the efforts to expunge the record, this situation could not be hidden from others in the law enforcement community. Because of this, I deduced that the chief was a very vindictive and power- oriented person. I did not relish the idea of being the instrument of his undoing if that's where this next step was going. It was obvious to me that Alena could not have devised the allegations or the story on her own. The mayor suspected the same but rightfully wanted to get to the bottom of things. I did my best to weasel out of this next phase of the assignment, but he convinced me of its necessity.

We agreed on a pretty healthy fee, and I proceeded to interview Alena, again away from the station. I took her through the findings of my simulation, and after a period of time, she finally flipped. She tearfully admitted that the captain and the chief had "hit on her" many times over the course of the past few years. She was smart enough to avoid a physical entanglement with either of them but acknowledged that her rejections had caused some animosity to develop.

She told me that the captain had approached her about a month previously and said he had evidence that Alena's teenage son was involved in some illegal drug-related deal. The captain told her that he was gathering further evidence that would be used in a case against her son and threatened that her son could be facing serious jail time. Alena had feared for her son's safety and his future.

When confronted, Alena's son denied any drug-related involvement of any kind; he was a good student and a good boy. She believed him, went to the chief, and implored him to back the captain off as whatever evidence he was gathering was "trumped up." It was then that the chief told her that he would do that and also terminate the case against her son if she would do something for him. She expected that the chief was after sexual favors but found out that she was to participate in a plan to get rid of Sam. The chief outlined what he wanted Alena to do and say, and assured her that he would take care of the rest of the details. Once Sam was gone, so would the charges and case against her son.

I asked Alena to write up her statement and made sure she knew that she and her son would be protected. The mayor and I would handle the chief and the captain. There are very specific laws protecting whistleblowers from retaliation, and these laws would be in full force in this situation. While Alena participated in a conspiracy against Sam, there was enough justification to hold her harmless in its remedy.

Contacting the mayor, I filled him in on Alena's story, and he read her report of the incident. I told him I believed the story and suggested that he call an emergency meeting of the city council. They could go into closed session because this was a confidential personnel matter that must be addressed privately. State sunshine laws accommodate such private meetings. Normally all city or county government business is required by law to be conducted in a public setting, but exceptions are made for circumstances like these. The mayor was not hesitant or irresolute. In fact, he was energized. He anticipated that the captain and the chief were going down and felt his grandson was about to be vindicated.

That evening, an emergency closed session of the city council was held. I presented the findings of my investigation of the allegations against Sam and my meeting with Alena. My recommendation was that both the captain and the chief be terminated and Sam be placed as interim chief while the city conducted a search for a new one. In addition, I was willing to structure and facilitate the termination of the two conspirators and added that they had little choice in the face of this situation. The council members were horrified, and the political and legal consequences of terminating or not terminating were discussed throughout the meeting. In the end, the council voted to terminate the two and delegated the authority to me to structure and facilitate that action.

This was a very big leap of faith for the council, but not so much for the mayor. For him, the rat had been exposed and things were as they should be. There was much political angst and worry about the next steps. I assured them that I would handle the matter but also advised them that their values were on display with this and every decision that they made. The values displayed in the conspiracy against Sam could never be allowed to stand as a model for how things were done in that police department or that town. Urging them to take the high road, I suggested they had a fiduciary obligation to the citizens and a legal obligation to Alena and Sam. If they were going to be engaged in a battle, that battle should be on the side of what was right and what was just. The city would not need to embark on a legal battle, but rather the captain and the chief could be convinced that it was in their best interests to resign and move on. A legal battle would be public, slow and expensive. I felt that Alena would be a credible witness and very convincing should she be compelled to take the stand against the captain and chief. I gambled that they would realize how credible she would be and see the wisdom in backing down. High drama would unfold. The press and the city employees knew that something was happening because of the emergency closed meeting. Regardless, the chief and the captain anticipated that they would, as they had in the past, prevail.

The council and the mayor agreed to accept my recommendation and proposal to assist them in handling this mess. My first step was to telephone Sam and seek his approval to act as the interim chief. His cooperation was the linchpin of my plan. Without interim leadership, the department would be cast into chaos, which had to be avoided. The city could not be expected to operate without a functioning police department. Of course, Sam was startled by my call and asked if his wife could pick up the extension and listen in the conversation. I said yes. I told him that I had gotten to the bottom of the situation and relayed Alena's story and reasons for filing the false report that had endangered his job and career. He was not nervous. He was not tentative. One could feel the tension dissipate as he accepted the interim assignment as chief. It would begin tomorrow, and he was to wait for my call. I urged him to contact each of the police officers and administrative staff that evening and let them know of his interim assignment. A meeting would be held in the morning to provide clarification and details. I doubted that there would be any sleep had in any of those houses that night.

The mayor and I then went to the police station and asked the chief to meet with us privately, leaving the captain for the second meeting. I started the meeting by telling the chief that this could be a criminal matter, and if it were handled incorrectly or carelessly, it would probably result in the end of his career. You should've seen the expression on his face! He had expected me to be talking about Sam's job and career, not his. I told him that we had very credible testimony from Alena regarding the conspiracy he concocted against Sam. The chief denied everything, denounced Alena as a liar, and said this was simply an attempt to falsely blame him. He was vehement and excited, but fortunately the mayor's presence acted as a calming force.

I informed the chief that he would be lucky if he were only terminated. The mayor and the city could handle this case as a criminal matter, but they were not inclined to go in that direction. If he were terminated, he would never be able to work in law enforcement or supervision. The city had the resolve and the funds to mount a very credible civil case and such a case would be slow, painful and expensive for him. There would be no escape, no refuge, and the inevitable outcome would result in the total destruction of his career. I paused to let this soak in, as I wanted the chief to marinate in his future as I was laying it out. This was an important factor in setting up the negotiation that would follow.

Now I suggested to the chief that there was an alternative to the scenario I had presented and that there might be an opportunity to avoid the complete destruction of his professional life. Another long pause. I wanted this potential opportunity for redemption to begin to take shape in his mind. Continuing, I told him this alternative to public termination came with several conditions. At this point, the chief's head was spinning, and at this stage I understand that the person I'm talking to is not really capable of addressing the micro aspects of any potential deal I might have to offer. The chief was focused on the macro aspects of the ending of his career and his life as he had known it. Given this reality, there was no point to attempt to outline the parameters of any deal. My objective was to end the meeting with a stern warning urging that the chief not do or say anything that might be considered provocative or in any way endanger his position or opportunity to avoid termination. It had to be completely clear that he "was hanging by a thread." He had done so much wrong in the past, now was the time to start doing things right. I advised him that we were going to have a similar conversation with the captain and that no safe harbor would be found there. The chief was told not to contact anybody on the force, not to use his computer to remotely access information, and not to use city property or assets. I told him to go home and meet with me in the morning to discuss the details associated with an alternative. It was a very powerful meeting.

Our next meeting was with the captain, and it was essentially the same meeting we had had with the chief. He too was obstreperous and cocky at first. My objective was to end the meeting with the same warning and request as I had given to the chief. We would meet tomorrow and discuss the city's choices and his future.

The mayor and I then returned to the council members. Even thought the meeting was over, they were still assembled and, as one could guess, anxious to find out where things stood. The mayor brought them up to speed and urged them to go home, not speak to the media, and let tomorrow unfold. They did. Sam was called back and advised to place the calls to his full staff. They should not be allowed to exist "in the dark" even overnight. The police department functions 24 hours a day, and at no time should it be allowed to exist in ambiguity or chaos. While we hoped the captain and the chief would follow the directions provided to them, we could not be certain that they would comply. It could be possible that they would begin to formulate and mount a defense and start to coalesce support on their behalf. This was a very precarious point in the unfolding of events. The officers in the department had to be assured that there was stability within the department and legitimate leadership moving forward. They also needed to be warned not to allow themselves to be drawn into the controversy with the chief and the captain.

The mayor made himself available to Sam, now the new acting chief, during the formal meetings that followed each shift the next day. I busied myself with preparations for my meetings with the chief and the captain. Late morning of the next day, I called the chief and scheduled our first meeting for one o'clock. I then called the captain and scheduled his meeting for 3:30 pm. I never allow these meetings to become marathons. Two hours is the maximum amount of time, at one sitting, to get productive conversation. Everybody reacts differently in these meetings. The smart ones realize that when they're angry, they say things that harm their position or reveal more than should be revealed. The chief was angry, but coy. The captain was blustery and obnoxious.

Referring back to Elisa Kubler-Ross's work, *On Death and Dying,* about the five stages associated with accepting death, I find that her work can apply to helping people like this chief of police and his captain accept the death of their jobs. How many stages people go through and how quickly is determined by their personality and the situation. As the situation changes, so can the progress through the stages, which is what happened in this case. Sam went through the first two and stopped due to the allegations being false. For the chief and the captain, stages three through five came more into play.

The first stage in what Kubler-Ross describes as the grief cycle is denial, a conscious or unconscious refusal to accept facts and information or reality relating to the situation. It's a defense mechanism and perfectly natural. Some people can become locked in this stage when dealing with traumatic change. For Sam, it was denial that it could be happening; it was so far from his reality.

The second stage Kubler-Ross labels anger, and it can manifest itself in different ways. People dealing with emotional upset can be angry with themselves and/or with others, especially those close to them. Anger focused within can look like depression to the rest of us and could be described as an implosion. Anger focused at others could be described as an explosion. Once Sam realized he had been set up, anger set in. He could not really externalize his anger since the causes and targets of it were his bosses. Sam imploded and experienced the visceral and mental problems that accompanied it.

This second stage was the most challenging for me in my role in this case. It was during this stage that the chief and his captain were the most threatening and defiant which was directly affecting Sam. Remember that these people carry guns, are not afraid of using them and are used to running over the law. They come out of an environment where power from the chain of command trumps good judgment, fairness, or being right. This stage intuitively called for me to be stronger and more aggressive than the chief or the captain. In situations like this, I have found that strength exhibited in a "one down" style works better than "one upsmanship." This is not a time to be bigger or stronger. This is the time to be firmer and smarter. They would need to realize they were "caught" and be calm as they were about to experience stages three through five.

The third stage is bargaining. As a result of my intervention, Sam did not have to go through this stage; he was innocent and had no deals to make. Whether a person is an introvert or an extrovert, the bargaining stage is about trying to get a better deal. I had to convince two extroverts that their "blue wall" had crumbled and they were no longer in charge. The strength play from stage two worked, and I was able to get them to listen and understand the seriousness of the situation and the benefit to them of voluntary resignation.

Stage four is depression. In Kubler-Ross' work, this could be a dress rehearsal or a practice run simulating death. It's natural to feel sadness, regret, fear, and uncertainty. It shows that the person has begun to accept reality. The chief and the captain obviously were not happy campers at this point. They were now fully aware of the possible consequences for their actions and the heavy weight they would bear with the loss of their jobs and careers. One could say that while they were unhappy, they were also fully mindful of their position.

The final stage is acceptance. In Kubler-Ross' world, this is the stage when the individual is ready to die. In my world, this is where the individual is ready to sign the agreement, accept the settlement and move on. The chief and the captain voluntarily resigned.

This case concluded with a pretty happy ending. Sam was promoted from acting chief to permanent chief within 10 months. Dealing with the former chief and his captain was no picnic, but the end result was that they not only voluntarily resigned but signed hold harmless agreements as well. They got small severance packages and agreed to leave town. The mayor's hunch turned out to be right only there were two rats, not one, and immature ones at that. Their childish vendetta almost cost them their careers.

Management Lessons

1. When the leader of an organization or a work team is the problem, there is almost no hope of fixing the problem from the bottom up. In this case, the captain and the chief displayed moral bankruptcy and corruption. The leader's misbehavior can often tear at the actual fabric of the organization as the climate of any organization is generally directly related to its leaders.

2. There are many styles of management or leadership. There is one-upsmanship, and then there is one-downsmanship. One-upsmanship is where a person leads from solely a position of power and uses that power to dominate others. One-downsmanship is leadership that is expressed in a far more modest manner. It is not about domination but about leading from the back of the line. The captain. and the chief operated from the former style whereas the lieutenant led by example, thus demonstrating the latter style. The former style could be described as "It's my way or the highway," while the latter style is more "We're all in this together."

3. Sunshine laws and exemptions to sunshine laws were referenced in this chapter, and they exist in every state. They require public entities like local government and municipal operations, because they operate with public monies, to operate transparently. The public, since it provides the operating funds through taxes, has a right to view and participate in the decisions that the entity makes. Private enterprises like for-profit organizations can make decisions privately and without public input. Sunshine laws prohibit governments and other public institutions from behaving that way. Meetings of city councils or county commissioners can only be

held following public notification and allowing public observation. There are a few exceptions within sunshine laws allowing for decisions to be made in private. Most of those exceptions revolve around decisions that affect individual employees.

4. Hold harmless agreements are formal agreements made between employers and employees. The hold harmless agreement states that the employee agrees to take no action against the employer and to say nothing that is derogatory or may harm the organization in the public's eye. Additionally, the employer agrees to take no action that would harm the employee and agrees to say nothing (usually in a reference check) that would harm the employee's reputation or status with a prospective employer. These agreements can also be called waivers. The employee and the employer agree to waive their rights to seek redress against the other party.

Chapter 5

Unethical Acts and Contentious Boards: The County Health Department — the Hatfields and the McCoys

I received a call from the chairman of the board, Lynn, of a county health department. She advised me that there was a significant mess, and she desperately needed my help getting things sorted out. I asked for the broad-brush overview. She said the board was deeply divided, uncertain about the facts, and chaos was ruling. The county could not afford to have the health department be dysfunctional. There was no hospital in their county, and the citizens relied upon the county health department for most of their primary care.

Lynn told me there had been a mass resignation almost a month ago. Four of the six nurses on staff had resigned without notice, leaving patient care to suffer. It was unclear exactly why the resignations had occurred, but obviously something very wrong had happened. There was an informal but specific allegation that the executive director, Sharon, fired the director of nurses, Hannah, and replaced her with the executive director's future daughter-in-law. The general allegation was that Sharon lacked the skill and judgment to effectively operate the county health department. Lynn realized that the department was on the verge of collapse and that the state department of health could step in and shut them down. Worse yet, due to the shortage of staff, quality patient care was being threatened which could produce conditions which could precipitate lawsuits and bad PR. My experience told me she was correct and that the direction the health department was going was extremely serious.

I told her that I preferred to draft a thorough proposal first. A detailed scope document would minimize confusion and misunderstanding. Within it, I would identify the present situation and document my understanding of the context of the case The next element of my proposal would be an articulation of my objectives and the assumptions, as well as a section specifying the work delineated in my plan of action. The final section of the proposal would be entitled "Time, Staff, and Costs." In addition to detailing my timetable for starting and finishing a project, my proposals always include who, if anyone besides myself, will be working on the case as well as the fee I intend to charge. Lynn appreciated my intention to be orderly and specific but said the situation was so dire that I needed to be there tomorrow. Understanding, I told her that I would work on the proposal that day, and if she approved it, would change my schedule to meet with her the next day, long drive notwithstanding.

I have found that because most of my work is addressing a crisis, my clients don't care or worry too much about my fees at the beginning, or even about my understanding of the situation. They just want me to intercede as quickly as possible. I always go back to that first management tenant of never making a bigger mess than the one in which you find yourself. I've also found that once things settle down, the scope of my work and fees will then become a focus of conversation. The last thing I want or need, or my clients' want or need, is for me to contribute to the chaos or their pain. I need to come into the case with clarity and purpose, so I insist upon drafting thorough scope documents and having the client approve my work plan in writing.

With these documents in hand, Lynn and I met at the health department. I discovered she was a retired nurse who seemed honest, sincere, and very credible. Agreeing to my proposal, she signed the engagement letter formally authorizing me to enter the case. She told me her version of the entire situation, admitting that several holes existed in her understanding of all the aspects and elements of the mess. My work plan, directly from my proposal, included:

Step 1.   The consultant will interview, by phone or in person, all members of the board and obtain their insights about the problems in the organization from the board's perspective.

Step 2.   The consultant will meet with and interview the staff persons making allegations or expressing concerns regarding what is happening at the health department.

Step 3.   The consultant will meet with and interview the staff person or persons about whom allegations have been made to gather perspectives on incidents. Additionally, instructions will be provided to assure that no retaliation for the allegations occurs.

Step 4.   The consultant may interview past employees to gather their perspective on matters present at the health department.

Step 5.   The consultant will analyze and synthesize the information and insights gathered from the interviews and form an opinion regarding the severity of the situation and the appropriate steps to address the current organizational climate.

Step 6.   The consultant will provide an oral report of findings with conclusions and recommendations for an appropriate response to the findings to the board for their consideration.

I began by making appointments and then speaking with the other six board members, five women and one man. The man was a pharmacist in town, one of the women was the wife of the local veterinarian, and another woman was an accountant in town. The other three women on the board were high school educated and otherwise unremarkable. The mayor of the town appointed all board members for multi-year terms.

As I interviewed each board member to ascertain his or her assessment of the situation, I found myself recognizing the difference between formally educated and less educated people. It would be interesting to see if this experience mirrors or contradicts your own view if you have ever considered the matter yourself. My view is that people who do not have a formal education tend to view things as black and white, this way or that, right or wrong. People with a formal education beyond high school tend to see things more in shades of gray. Not trying to be elitist but practical in viewing the differences, I have found people with a formal post-secondary education tend to look at problems and see four or five different alternatives. Then, they identify the best one. On the contrary, people with only a high school education tend to look at the same problem and see the one right or the one wrong alternative.

I'm reminded of a movie from early 1992 called *A River Runs Through It*. You may recall the movie was somewhat about fly-fishing, but there was a very salient theme that I identified. Remember the part in the movie where the father, who was home schooling his son, gave his son the assignment to write a paper? I do not remember the subject of the paper, but I do remember that after the son wrote it and turned it into his father, he read it and told his son to go back and rewrite it. The son dutifully rewrote the paper and again gave it to his father. Once again, his father read the paper and advised his son to rewrite and resubmit. For the third time, the son rewrote the paper and gave it to his father. His father was finally satisfied with the paper, and in front of his son, he crumpled it up and threw it away. Then he told his son that he could now go fishing. What that scene revealed to me was the essence of formal higher education. The student is asked to articulate his or her feelings or findings on some subject matter. The professor rejects it and advises the student to try again. The professor again forces the student to rethink and restate his or her position, feelings, or findings to be clearer or more specific. It's the learning process that is as important, if not more, than the content.

Getting back to the case, the three board members without formal education after high school saw things very differently than the college-educated members. This will unfold more dramatically as this chapter continues. Basically, the board was completely polarized four to three. It was like the Hatfields and the McCoys. The McCoys saw the executive director as a saint. From their perspective, Sharon was a great executive director. The Hatfields saw her as a good person but also as the source of the problems. My job was to get to the bottom of the allegations that would reveal whether the Hatfields or the McCoys were correct.

I got the impression that several board members, the McCoys, did not like me very much. They saw me as an intruder, an interloper, and someone from the big city sticking his nose where he didn't belong. Funny how that happens. There's an old expression in the South relating to people from the North moving to the South — they never become Southerners. They say, "Just cause a cat has kittens in the oven, it don't make them biscuits." As far as the McCoys were concerned, outsiders were not to be trusted.

After completing the board interviews, I proceeded to interview all current staff members. I found the staff members curiously polarized. About half of the staff loved Sharon and supported her unequivocally, while the other half thought she was a complete idiot as an administrator. I learned that she did terminate the beloved director of nurses, Hannah. I say beloved because all staff members were in agreement that Hannah was highly respected, both as a person and as a medical practitioner. To add insult to the situation, Sharon had then hired her future daughter-in-law to become the new director. The future daughter-in-law was a registered nurse with experience in home healthcare, but the nursing staff was incensed that this person was placed in this role at Hannah's expense. In protest of this action, three staff nurses immediately resigned without notice, plunging the nursing function into chaos and a situation of being severely short-staffed.

Now Sharon was also a registered nurse. She immediately placed herself in the role of one of the nursing staff in an attempt to operate the department. She, her future daughter-in-law, and the one remaining staff nurse worked the home healthcare duties of the health department. Remember that the original nursing department struggled to keep up with four registered nurses and was now operating with three. And Sharon, functioning as a registered nurse, was neglecting her duties as administrator.

To make matters worse Sharon, while at home one evening, literally shot herself in the foot while cleaning a rifle. She blew the great toe on her right foot clean off. Because of the staffing caseload and shortage of personnel, Sharon hobbled on her injured foot and continued to see patients and provide home healthcare instead of resting. As a result, some on the board and in the community saw her as a hero of patient care and a living, shining example of service to the county.

I interviewed Hannah and the three nurses who had voluntarily terminated in protest. Each individual was conflicted about the situation. They knew that their patients were suffering, the health department's status with the state was precarious, and that they were being demonized in some quarters. They were also resolute in their view that they were right and what the executive director did had been very wrong. Two of the nurses had new jobs lined up and were glad to leave the health department, and Hannah and the other nurse indicated their willingness to come back under the right circumstances.

Working around the staff interviews, I spent a few days examining all the business aspects of the health department's operations. This included looking at the HR systems, job descriptions, performance appraisal system, policy and procedure manual, and the compensation system. I also looked at the budget and financial controls and was appalled to find that these areas were in a complete state of disarray. It turned out that the only thing that functioned properly was the nursing service.

In my report of findings, I wrote my investigation had substantiated the general allegation that Sharon lacked the administrative skills needed to operate the health department. I also substantiated the specific allegation that she did inappropriately and without cause terminate Hannah. The report stated:

In the financial arena:

The executive director appears not to be very adept at understanding or using financial information. She did not know the amount of the fund balance or the actual amount of the operating budget of the health department. The budget development and operations process is primarily handled by the bookkeeper. Understanding and operating the financial aspects of the department's budget is a crucial skills set. The ED did not know that the fund balance was in excess of $226,000. She thought it was around $90,000. The ED could not tell me the amount of the health department's annual budget. She did, to her credit, have an approximate notion of the budget's monthly total indicating that it was around $54,000 per month. Actually, it was $55,681 per month. She indicated that she reviewed the budget every quarter and started working on the new budget in the final quarter of the year.

Understanding and using financial information in the daily, weekly, monthly, and annual operation of the health department is essential in the current environment. Spotting and reacting to financial trends, monitoring cash flow, management and maximization of investments, management of cash, and accounts payables and receivables is all the domain of the director.

In the leadership, management, and ethical arenas:

Even the staff who supported the ED acknowledged that she was "too nice" and that she tried to be a buddy and please everyone. Feedback confirmed that she approved requests for leave without checking the impact of the absences on the schedule. Her leave approvals left staffing short. Feedback exists from two aides who, for a period of time, had patients and clients who required seven day per week visits. This weekend burden was falling on two aides, and when they asked for help so that they did not have to cover all the weekends, nobody would volunteer to assist with the coverage. They approached the ED for leadership and were told that since nobody wanted to help them, they would have to cover it for themselves.

Another confirmed incident that demonstrated a lack of leadership and management expertise was a situation in which two staffers were engaged in a shouting match in which personal attacks occurred. The ED was present, observed the unprofessional exchange, and failed to call a halt to, or deal with, the situation.

Her supporters and detractors indicated that she was gone too much. It could be said that she was away attending meetings in order to keep up with industry trends and governmental expectations, but much of the feedback indicated that she was away dealing with migraine headaches and recovering from the gun accident. Feedback from several staff indicated that the ED stated publicly and on several occasions that "her give-a-damn button was busted." This gives the impression of the presence of burnout, which suggests an explanation for the frequent absences. In any case, making such statements doesn't instill confidence.

The most serious issue to surface was a statement made by a staff person that Sharon pushed Hannah out of her position so that the future daughter-in-law could have the job. I spoke with Hannah and she confirmed that Sharon had come to her and said that her future daughter-in-law wished to come on staff at the health department. Hannah stated to me that she very clearly and precisely told Sharon that she wanted no part of the interview process and would have no role in bringing the future daughter-in-law on staff. From this point forward, Hannah continued, she felt stress and pressure from Sharon. If this happened, and it appears that it did, it represented a serious breach in ethics. Several at the health department perceived that it did happen.

With the hiring and promoting of future daughter-in-law to the position of second in charge, there was a coalition that effectively prevented any sort of accountability at the top. Staff could not complain or voice concerns to Sharon about the future daughter-in-law, and staff could not complain or voice concerns to future daughter-in-law about Sharon. The power of nepotism trumped accountability, which violated ethics principles and created a clear conflict of interest.

Several staff indicated that clients had complaints about the care future daughter-in-law provided and about the accuracy of her charting. These complaints went nowhere because of the future daughter-in-law's protected status. There was nothing in her personnel record about any conversations, warnings, or investigations into any accusations of wrongdoing. Complaints about the care provided, the care not provided, and the charting completed by a staff nurse are serious. Sharon should have reviewed them and future daughter-in-law should have been formally cleared or formally reprimanded. Neither happened.

I reviewed the staff's personnel records and discovered several problems. Among them, in every file reviewed, health records were co-mingled with other records. This was a clear violation of US Department of Labor regulations that specify that health-related records on employees shall be held confidential and cannot be co-mingled with any other records. Confidentiality or the lack thereof was a problem in the health department. Feedback confirmed that visitors of staff were allowed to come into the private offices of staff where patient records were clearly visible. All incoming mail was opened, thus allowing for personal records of staff to be viewed by the person opening mail. These examples indicated the lack of attention Sharon demonstrated to preserve confidentiality within the health department.

Another incident occurred and was verified by several staff persons. Sharon received a notice on January 30 from one of the state granters reminding the health department that its first quarter report (regarding the status of the grant activity) was due the next day. This was ignored. Two weeks later, the health department received a notice from the state indicating that the report had not been received and demanding it must be received at the state office immediately. This created a panicked response. The new staff person (responsible for the program) asked Sharon for help and learned that Sharon really did not know the answers nor did she understand the seriousness of the situation. This staff person worked with other staffers who gathered the information and got the report completed and submitted. The staff person had known about the January 30 reminder Sharon had received. Just for "grins" as well as possibly curiosity, the staffer commented to her that she thought it was very strange that the state would demand the report with no notice. Sharon told the staffer that she failed to understand the state's behavior either. So much for leadership.

This situation raised several "red flags" in the health department:

1. This denial or lack of acknowledgement regarding the January 30 reminder memo caused trust issues to be raised. The employee told me that she could have accepted an explanation like "I just completely forgot about the report being due; it slipped through the cracks." Even an honest "I blew it." would have been a sufficient answer. Instead, the ED's choice to omit or deny the truth caused her credibility to be reduced in the eyes of the staff.

2. Another red flag related to the ED's inability to understand the state's contract and its expectations is that this staff person realized that it is very significant to miss state program deadlines and to "mess with state money."

Conclusions:

There was clearly a mutiny at the health department as evidenced by the polarized staff. The outward signs of the mutiny occurred in November of the previous year. My hunch told me that it really started approximately 12 to 18 months prior. Feedback from several staff indicated that things had not been good at the department for about two years. I was not enamored by all the staff who were the Sharon's detractors. Even though they were on the right side of the issue, incompetence and incompatibility reigned at a level that could be dangerous to the health department's operations. Some of them were very credible, but some seemed to be snipers and snakes. These feelings aside, experience with these types tells me that complainers and snipers do not complain nor do they mutiny about nothing. It is always about something. Sharon failed to take the necessary steps to mitigate the discontent. Actually, she did much to foster it. Any of the above transgressions were enough to throw her credibility into question. Taken together, all clearly indicated that her status as executive director was unsalvageable and irreconcilable. I did not wish to see one side "win" and another side "lose." I saw plenty to convince me that all sides were hurting, patient care could be suffering, and the credibility and reputation of the health department was taking a hit. Changes were required.

General recommendations:

- Regarding the health department, it needs proper governance structure, internal leadership and teamwork, and human resources tools to operate the personnel.
- Regarding the community, it needs its health department to settle and operate ethically, orderly and efficiently ASAP.
- Regarding the director, I recommend she step aside and the board conduct a search for a new director.
- Regarding the staff, they need to be managed and held accountable for their performance.
- Regarding the board, you need to manage and educate yourselves regarding your highest and best role as the governing body.

Specific recommendations:

Regarding the board:

1. Job descriptions for board member and board chair are needed so that the roles of each are clearly defined.
2. A narrowly defined set of bylaws are needed or needs to be updated specifying how the board operates. The board should never allow its meetings to be dominated or captured by staff or public. The board meetings must be structured and disciplined so that it can conduct health department business.
3. An annual, or at least every other year, patient/client opinion survey should be conducted so that structured listening can be accomplished.
4. A subtle but concentrated PR campaign needs to be undertaken to assure the county leaders that the health department is back under control.

Regarding the executive director:

1. She should be replaced.
2. An interim director should be recruited and placed so that leadership, management, and healing can occur during the active search for the next director.

Regarding the health department:
Human resources tools need to be designed and put in place. They include the following:

1. A comprehensive policy manual
2. Job descriptions
3. An appraisal program
4. A wage and salary plan
5. Training on how to use the tools

This was just phase one of this assignment. The board and I had a rather contentious meeting to discuss the report delineated above. In the end, the three board members, the McCoys, voted to reject my report and proposal. The other board members, the Hatfields, chose to accept the proposal and asked me to assist them with phase two which would be the termination of Sharon and the restructuring of the health department. The not so unusual thing was that my investigation and report seemed to have no effect on the McCoys. When confronted with the conclusions, which I had drawn based upon extensive interviews, these board members chose to completely disregard everything, even though the facts were in front of them.

Remember the three to four board member split, as it will become very important as the case unfolds. The three McCoy board members represented the pro-administrator group. Four board members, the Hatfields, accepted my report as corroboration of their assessment of Sharon.

I outlined the work plan I intended to implement in phase two. We agreed that I would stay on site for approximately one to two weeks. My objective was to have as many meetings with Sharon as needed to either terminate her or obtain her voluntary resignation. Additionally, I would dig into the administrative matters that had been neglected during the period of time when Sharon acted as a staff nurse. I suggested one of my associates be considered as the interim executive director. He had the time and the administrative expertise to assure the board and the state that the health department would be operated safely and effectively. While he acted as the interim ED, he could also conduct the search for a permanent replacement. Again on a four to three vote, the board accepted my proposal.

Phase two proceeded fairly smoothly in some ways, but in other ways, it continued to act like the "Wild Wild West." The home health nursing and patient care demands on the schedule were extensive. Full staff consisted of four nurses and only three were immediately available. Sharon, her future daughter-in-law, and one other nurse were providing the patient care coverage. Bringing back Hannah and the other staff nurse who had left under protest but still available, was under consideration but problematic. The questions remained: Could the decision to roll back the termination of the previous director of nurses be made? Answer yes. Could the decision to roll back the hiring of the future daughter-in-law be made? Answer: questionable. Could the existing nurses work with the terminated nurses? Answer: questionable. The odds that things would work out ranked right up there with winning the lottery. Should that happen, however, the two nurses, Hannah and the self-terminated registered nurse, could replace Sharon and fill the vacant position.

Newsflash — it's next to impossible to win the lottery! By this time, the registered nurse had taken another job. Hannah agreed to come back at her previous salary but in the role of a staff nurse. On a more controversial note, Sharon agreed to voluntarily resign, but wanted to stay on as a staff nurse for an eight-week period at the same salary. While working, she would use the eight weeks to conduct a job search for her next position. Satisfying the home health patient's requirements for treatment superceded almost all other considerations. This eight-week contract bought the board two month's time to recruit and select a replacement staff nurse. This provided yet another example of what a saint Sharon had been! Also, a cool down period was under way which facilitated staff morale and the rebuilding of the health department.

So this is where we stood two weeks into phase two: Sharon had resigned, signed the hold harmless waiver, and accepted a time-specific contract in which she acted as a staff nurse. Patient care needs were being satisfied, and the state was cautiously happy. I was working on job descriptions and developing a policy and procedure manual for the health department, and my recommendation for the interim executive director had been accepted. The chairman of the board had already interviewed him by telephone, was satisfied with his credentials, and ready to approve his formal start the day after the upcoming board meeting.

The board meeting was scheduled, the interim ED had been selected, and all that remained was the formal authorization to proceed – or so I thought. The media had been all over the story for the previous two months, and the community had attended the board meetings over the past several months and been quite vocal in their support for or against Sharon and the board's actions. Sharon's two brothers had actually stopped by the health department on one occasion and threatened me. I assured them that the situation with their sister was well under control and operating to a great extent in her favor and instructed them to communicate with her for confirmation. I further communicated to them that if they threatened me again, I would press assault charges — the big oafs.

The board meeting rolled around and brought some surprises. The media was there, the community was there in mass, and Sharon's brothers were there. Staff members were present, as well as the interim director and myself. None of these were surprises. I asked one of the staff to call the county sheriff and ask that he be present at the meeting for crowd control. He arrived, took out his gun in clear view, and took a seat. What was a surprise was that Lynn, the chairman of the board, was not present. She had been called out of town due to a last-minute family emergency. The vice chair, a pharmacist by training and a rather fragile looking little person physically, convened the meeting. As soon as he had called the meeting to order, one of the board members, a McCoy, immediately began a verbal attack on his character. I halfway expected an attack on me. Even though I had accomplished all of the goals specified in the proposal for phase two, I never expect a pat on the back, but rather someone to be there with a kick to my derrière. What I did not expect was the personal attack of one board member on another.

It was a brutal attack. A second member of the McCoy group picked up the club and continued the attack on the pharmacist. It seemed to come out of nowhere, but I finally figured out what was occurring. What the McCoy clan of the board was attempting to accomplish, through this diatribe, was to get the vice chairman to become so incensed or embarrassed that his fight or flight reflex would overtake him, and he would resign on the spot. If he did resign, that would leave five members present at this board meeting and they would represent a 3 to 2 voting bloc. With this majority, the McCoy clan could vote to terminate the consultant's contracts and reinstate Sharon. Talk about political drama! I had to admit it was a pretty savvy move by the McCoys. I interceded to the greatest extent possible, but was shouted down by the McCoys and told that because I was not a board member, I did not have the right to speak. I whispered in the pharmacist's ear to remain calm and to remain seated. It took all of his will and all of my effort to keep his backbone erect. I practically ordered this board member to do nothing, stay strong, and allow the attack to roll off his back. This was an attempted coup, and he could defeat it by letting them run out of steam and simply thank them for their comments. By ignoring the content, he could sidestep the context and win this battle.

The pharmacist stood firm, and the coup failed. Fortunately, the sheriff was present to maintain order in the public gallery. It was all pretty exciting but when I stop to think about it, it was pretty depressing. The McCoy members embarked on an exercise that would basically rip at the fabric of the whole organization. Remember how important the health department was to its patients and the county in general. The McCoys' actions would have served to return the department to total chaos, which could only have resulted in patient care breakdown and forced the state to step in and either take it over or shut it down. Everything that I had accomplished, and they had paid for, would have been undone.

In the end, the interim executive director's contract was approved, and the plan that I had established was carried out. I was vilified by some, and recognized by almost none. Lynn appreciated my work, but by not being at the meeting, she was left "rolling her eyes" at the thought of what could have happened. This had been a close call due to her unexpected absence; it could have all come crashing down. The interim executive director conducted an effective search and within three months a qualified, competent, and experienced ED was selected. The Hatfields and the McCoys still existed, side-by-side, on the board. As the health department settled down and became functional, the media and the community also calmed down and normalcy returned, as it should. The steady state of any organization should be peace. My role had been that of a wartime officer, so I was just as happy to leave that health department, as the McCoys were to see me go.

Management Lessons

1. There is a difference in the way people think and do problem-solving depending upon their education. People who have a formal education at the college level and beyond think differently than the folks with only a high school education. A college education fundamentally teaches people that there are multiple solutions for any problem, and college-educated people understand that their objective is to identify the best solution among many possibilities. Folks that only have a high school education tend to see a problem as having a right or a wrong answer. A formal education beyond high school forces the person to examine a situation from a wide variety of perspectives. Few people, without the benefit of higher education, can discipline themselves to think that way. Management should attempt to hire employees with a college education for positions that require problem solving and should try to provide training in problem solving to employees with no post-secondary education.

2. In this case, I identified an ethics breach. When the administrator fired the director of nurses and hired her future daughter-in-law, it was an unethical act. It is significant to note that for something to be called or described as ethical, it must meet a

two-pronged definition: it must *be* and *look* ethical to be called ethical. Something that is actually ethical, but doesn't look ethical doesn't qualify. Something that has the appearance of being ethical but actually isn't ethical cannot be called ethical. A conflict of interest could certainly be an ethics breach. For example, a not-for-profit executive director recommended that the board of the organization purchase some land for expansion purposes. However, the executive director did not disclose the fact that he was part owner of that land. On the surface, his recommendation *looked* ethical when, in actuality, it was not.

3. The US Department of Labor requires employers to maintain two separate files for employee records. The file that contains health-related records must be kept segregated or separated from all other employee records (that may include contact information and performance review information). Health-related records are also required to be segregated and housed separately from other employee information kept by the employer. This gets back to the priority that the DOL places on health-related matters in the workplace. Not only should there be two separate files, the one containing the health-related information must have a higher level of confidentiality.

Chapter 6

Cultural Differences: A Tale of Two Thresholds

"A Tale of Two Thresholds" is actually two cases, similar but, at the same time, so different that I thought it would be interesting to present them together. While they are both sexual harassment cases, they take place in different settings and represent two ends of the spectrum regarding what is offensive and what is not. As stated, the criteria for determining sexual harassment is the question: Would a reasonable woman find this behavior offensive? If the answer is yes, you probably have sexual harassment. If the answer is no, you probably don't. Notice the qualifier "probably."

The first case took place in a large university. I received a call from the provost, which in university-speak, is the chief operating officer (COO). The provost, Marcus, said that a graduate student in the physics department had made an allegation of sexual harassment. Since we had a retainer arrangement, I was able to get on site quickly and start the investigation as the 72-hour clock had begun to run. Again, the law requires the employer organization to begin an investigation within 72 hours of being notified of the allegation of sexual harassment. I made arrangements to be on campus the next day.

Shortly after my arrival on campus, the provost met with me. Under normal circumstances, I would have prepared a thorough proposal outlining my understanding of the present situation, my objectives, assumptions, work plan, timetable, and proposed fee. In this case, I had a retainer relationship with the client and the front-end scope documents that I require in all cases had already been prepared and agreed upon. This client organization is so big that allegations appear fairly regularly. You may be wondering why allegations of misbehavior, sexual harassment or otherwise, would occur regularly in a large organization like a university. They had enacted a comprehensive sexual harassment prevention strategy but still had regular sexual harassment (and other misbehavior) allegations. Why? A university campus, by design, is a promiscuous and open environment. By promiscuous I don't mean immoral, but rather an environment that encourages experimentation, not with substances but with ideas. There are many freedoms built into the environment that make it artificial compared to the typical business setting. This particular school had 23,000 students and 6,000 faculty and staff. If 1% is a "bad apple," that's still a big number!

So, I was in the provost's office gaining my first understanding regarding the details of the allegation. To be candid, they were a bit skimpy. The allegation was that the male chairman (dean) of the physics department asked a female graduate student to accompany him to lunch. The female graduate student filed a sexual harassment complaint immediately thereafter, and I was called in. That's all the provost knew.

I obtained the name and phone number of the graduate student, Raani, because I always start with the alleged victim. I called her, introduced myself and my role, and made an appointment for an interview. Raani insisted that the interview take place at the provost's office, to which I agreed and we met privately. After a second introduction, I gave her the standard introductory messages. This was a confidential personnel matter, and I was an independent third-party, only connected to the school as a private contractor. My role was to thoroughly understand the situation, make some assessments about its severity, and then make a report to the school. As always, I apologized in advance for the indelicate nature of the situation and explained that my questions were required to get to "the bottom of things."

Raani proceeded to tell me that she was a PhD student on a full scholarship provided by her home country, Pakistan. When she arrived at the beginning of the summer semester, she found out that the dean was out of the country for the entire summer, and she was offended that he was not going to be available to her for the first semester. I was beginning to see a sense of superiority and entitlement in this student's demeanor, which was not too surprising. She had already earned a doctoral degree in Pakistan and her school expenses were being provided by her government, which clearly indicated she was somebody. When you add all this up and couple it with the fact that she was a PhD level physics student, it's not hard to guess that she would be arrogant and abrasive. She told me that when the dean did arrive back on campus, his first contact with her was to invite her to lunch. She stared at me with anger burning in her eyes, her arms folded in, and her back erect. Her next question was, "Are all Americans sex maniacs?" I told her that I did not think so and asked her to proceed with the incident's details. She looked at me with an expression of incredulity on her face. Then she repeated that the dean had asked her to accompany him to lunch. That's what happened! I said I understood and then asked her what happened next. She told me that I obviously failed to understand her, and, once again, said, "That's what happened."

At the beginning of this chapter, I reviewed the criterion for defining sexual harassment, which is the question: Would a reasonable woman find this behavior offensive? To clarify her allegation, I again asked if the basis for making the complaint against the dean was that he invited her to lunch. She said yes, so naturally I asked her why that was so offensive. Again, with that same look of incredulity, she proceeded to tell me that she was a woman. I told her that my eyes were working; I could see that. With encouragement to proceed, she added that she was a married woman. I told her that I had noticed her wedding ring, but I still did not understand why an invitation to lunch was so offensive. Raani said she was a married, Pakistani woman and that, in her culture, an invitation from any man who was not her husband, her son, or her father, obviously had illicit intentions. In a rare moment for me, I let my professional guard down and blurted out, "Well Dorothy, you're not in Kansas anymore!" Obviously, she wasn't familiar with *The Wizard of Oz*. Now I had completely exasperated her.

I explained that, in this culture, an invitation to lunch was not necessarily a part of any immoral intention. Out of courtesy and respect, I told her that I would continue the investigation, but I knew that the criteria of "Would a reasonable woman find that behavior offensive?" probably would suggest that no sexual harassment had occurred. In addition, I told her that I recognized that she was offended that the dean was not available to her when she arrived on campus, and I wondered if those feelings might have clouded her judgment in this incident. Still convinced of her claim, Raani assured me that his invitation to lunch certainly was a part of his illicit intention, and she was justified and correct in her reading of the situation.

Next, I spent some time with Raani obtaining more background information regarding her culture. Since it was the source of her complaint, I wanted a thorough understanding of her background so I could see the situation from her point of view. I thanked her and assured her that I would get back with her regarding my findings. Asking her to put her feelings on hold for the moment, I requested that she attend classes normally and give me some time to complete my investigation without her taking any provocative steps — steps that might damage her position with the dean or the school. I believed she understood.

My next interview was with the dean whom I found to be introverted, yet very professional. The man had his doctorate in molecular physics and, while a little "bookish," was personable. He was completely dumbfounded by Raani's allegation that he sexually harassed her.

I asked him why he extended a personal invitation to Raani for lunch. He told me that the physics department was very small and that there were seven faculty members, each representing a different micro area of physics. All new graduate students at the doctoral level were interviewed to determine which area of physics they were most interested in pursuing. Once the student's interests were ascertained, he would make an assignment to the appropriate faculty member. The incoming PhD class was always small, as they accepted no more than 10 students per semester. The dean invited each of the new students to a luncheon as a way to get to know them and ascertain their specific interests in the field of physics. It was all very collegial and above board, and it was what he had attempted to do with Raani. He told me that this had been his practice for years and years, and there had never been an allegation of sexual harassment made against him or any of his faculty. Thanking him, I advised that I would be speaking with a few of his faculty members if he did not mind. He gave his permission, and the interview was over.

The secretary gave me a roster of the physics department's faculty, and I proceeded to interview two. They were also bookish, but I thought one was more outgoing than the other. I might've described him as a physics extrovert! Actually, there is a joke about physicists that, stereotypes aside, actually fit these two faculty members. Do you know how you can tell the physics extrovert from the physics introvert? The physics extrovert stares at your shoes when he's talking to you; whereas, the introvert stares at his own shoes when he's talking to you! Interviewing isn't always easy. Seriously though, both of these faculty members were very helpful and confirmed that the dean, for as long as they could remember, had invited the new doctoral students to lunch with the purpose of getting to know them and their specific interests in physics. They explained that a student with an interest in astral physics would be assigned to a different faculty advisor then a student with an interest in biological physics. The student would be required to take courses from the entire faculty, but their advisor would be the faculty member whose expertise was the most closely aligned to the student's principal area of interest.

Now that I had determined that the dean's behavior with Raani had been consistent with his behavior with all other doctoral students, my next stop was at the Center for Middle East Studies. I wanted to find out as much as I could about Raani's background. This was the nice part about working around the university: there were a lot of resources contained in one general area. After locating an expert on Pakistani culture, I told him, without revealing any names or any specifics of the case, that I was looking for specifics on a particular religious sect. When I told them the name of the sect, he instantly clapped his hands and rolled his eyes. He told me that, in Pakistan, the people that practiced their religion in this particular way were outlawed. They saw sex and sexuality in everything, symbolic or not. For example, they viewed the dome of a mosque as a breast, and the spire on it was seen as penis. He said they were nuts and were recognized as such throughout the Pakistani culture. Unbelievable! He told me that these people were zealots, and their minds were not open to reason, which is why law in Pakistan banned them.

I now felt like my investigation was complete. There was no sexual harassment, and from my point of view, the allegation was overturned. The dean would be exonerated, but I somehow anticipated that Raani wouldn't be satisfied. If she were the same kind of zealot that the professor of Middle Eastern studies had suggested, this wouldn't end here. I went to the provost, made my report, and suggested a rather radical course of action.

There are two governmental levels for departments of education, state and federal. Schools, along with other professional settings, have what is called a mandatory report requirement. If they suspect that a student has been abused, the law mandates them to self-report to either the state or the federal department. Other professionals like doctors and nurses are similarly mandated. If they suspect a patient has been abused, there is a law that mandates them, under penalty of losing their license, to report the suspected abuse to state authorities. Understanding this legal reality caused me to suggest to the provost that we self-report, a process called "hot -lining." I knew from my investigation that there was no sexual harassment, and I presumed that the state would come to the same conclusion. If Raani were dissatisfied with my conclusions, as I suspected she would be, her next recourse would be to report the incident to the state. Since we had confidence in my conclusions regarding what the state would decide with this allegation, self-reporting now would be a smart move. The school could "keep its powder dry" and still be exonerated. The student could be mad if she wanted to be, but her anger would be directed at the state instead of the school. Cool.

The provost agreed, called the state department of education, and hot-lined it himself! In my presence, he advised the director that a sexual harassment allegation had been made by a student against the dean of her department.

The director thanked him for his candor and said he would schedule an investigation to begin — you guessed it — within 72 hours.

The provost let the dean know that he had been hot-lined and also advised him of my findings and the strategy embedded in the decision to call the state. He was disconcerted but understood the plan. Raani was advised her that the state department of education had been notified, and that they would be on campus to complete their own investigation. This was a lot of drama for the physics department, but it couldn't be avoided. And, the drama that was unfolding turned out to have severe consequences for Raani.

In the end, what I had hoped, predicted, and planned actually came about. The state's investigation found no sexual harassment and effectively shut down any further opportunities for recourse. Unfortunately for Raani, she had done herself in. She had so ruined her relationship with the dean, the faculty, and the school, that she was forced to withdraw from the program. The graduate community, especially in fields like physics, is so small that most deans know each other, or feel close enough to place a phone call seeking information about the transfer of a student at the doctoral level. Raani, because she had filed a formal complaint of sexual harassment against the dean, unfortunately became radioactive. No other dean, in any other PhD level physics program at any university, would take a chance on her. She had to go back to her husband and government in disgrace for failing to complete her program. She was probably forced to repay the funds her government had expended up to the day of her withdrawal since she had signed a contract.

Okay, now let's contrast the case of the Pakistani woman with another case. This is the case of a 35-year-old female plumber's assistant employed in a small construction firm for about two and half years. In this case, the female employee, Abby, was not sexually harassed by her supervisor, the field superintendent — he had raped her. And, this was a serialized rape that occurred on multiple occasions over a two-year period of time. The superintendent, Dave, basically took this woman at work and during normal work hours, whenever he felt like it. When this situation finally came into public light, I asked Abby what she would like to see happen as a remedy. I told her that she could potentially have a criminal case of forcible rape, or she could have a civil case against this employee and the employer. Her preferred solution was to take no action against either the company or the superintendent but simply to obtain a cease and desist against the supervisor. I was startled by her position! She didn't even want her supervisor fired or charged civilly or criminally, just wanted him to leave her alone.

How could she take such a passive stance especially given the definition of harassment? How could rape be reasonable? Abby's response suggested that she could have been a willing partner, but then she said that she neither liked it nor wanted to do it; it was "only" a blowjob or "only" sex. She had not been a willing partner, but rather a weakling who had easily become a victim. With the synopsis of the case as background, let me now take you back to the beginning.

This was a small construction firm that had two crews operating under the supervision of one superintendent. It had been owned and operated by the same individual for most of his life. The owner had operated the company following what I would describe as the "BS and I" method which stands for brute strength and ignorance. He operated the business and the employees using the "my way or the highway" style of leadership additionally infused with chauvinism and crudeness. Since he was retiring, his son, a college-trained licensed civil engineer, had taken over the business.

His educated son, Ryan, was cognizant of laws associated with the department of labor and had an understanding of the changing workforce. He set out to operate the business in a more enlightened and professional way. Since there were several females employed in this construction company, I had been hired to conduct sexual harassment prevention training for the employees. It was after this training that Abby came forward and reported the abuse to Ryan, the new young president of the company.

Once the allegation was made, Ryan called me back to conduct an investigation. I went through my usual steps of developing scope documents and obtaining approvals to proceed. Once those steps were successfully completed, Ryan told me what Abby had alleged. He was clearly anxious as he recognized the potential severity of the charges that could fall on his newly acquired company.

I interviewed Abby and was provided with all the gory and unseemly details of incident after incident after incident. I asked her why she put up with this situation for so long and why she decided to report it now. She had several reasons. When all this started, she was married to an abusive alcoholic and responsible for supporting and protecting a teenage daughter. When she told her husband about the first incident, a request for oral sex, she said that he had backhanded her so hard that she flew across the room. He told her that if she ever did anything to encourage her boss again, he would beat her to death. She also told me that she didn't think that the owner would support her, as he was both a chauvinist and a philanderer. Abby said that she needed this job to support her daughter and herself and had decided she would just have to take the bad with the good. I asked her how it all started and how she responded to the initial demands for sex. She told me that he came up to her, put his arm around in a hold that wouldn't allow her to squirm away, and then asked for oral sex. She tried to treat it as a joke, but when he persisted, she eventually cried while begging him to leave her alone. He threatened to fire her if she didn't cooperate, so she then resigned herself to the necessity to cooperate in order to keep her job.

Abby endured this for two years, finally coming to me when I was there for the sexual harassment prevention training. She asked me to take it to Ryan for her. Her situation at the time of the allegation was that she had divorced and been rid of the alcoholic husband for a year. Her daughter had graduated high school and was now on her own, and there was a new president of the company who seemed like someone who would support her. Because of the training I had provided, she now knew her rights. These things constituted sufficient change for her to seek an improvement in her circumstances.

I also learned that she had mentioned this situation to the company engineer almost a year ago, but when he didn't seem to get it or take any action, she took it as a sign that things were just going to continue the way they were. I was blown away by the report from this victim. Normally, my second interview would be with the alleged perpetrator, but not in this case. This case was so outrageous that I went directly to the engineer and asked him if he remembered the conversation Abby had referred to. He said that he did not remember the specifics of the conversation, but he did say he remembered that she had approached him about something. He acknowledged that he had not understood what she was trying to say and had let it go.

My next interview was with the superintendent, Dave. I went through my usual introduction indicating that this was a confidential personnel matter and that I was seeking his candid and honest cooperation regarding the allegations made against him. He told me he understood, and I proceeded with specific questions. I asked him about the allegation; he denied everything. He denied ever having sex or demanding sex from this employee. Dave was physically big, standing about six foot five and weighing over 200 pounds. He was used to barking orders and unused to answering questions. I told him that I would continue my investigation whether he liked it or not and advised him to take no action that might be considered provocative or might meet the definition of retaliation. I told him the law was very specific in its protections against retaliation of whistleblowers.

There was one other female, Jill, on the construction crew. She was the electrician's assistant who was eight years on the job and about two years away from earning her status as a journeyman electrician. She, like Abby, was slight in stature but different from her in that she had a very direct and strong demeanor.

I informed her that I needed her assistance in a confidential personnel matter and asked her to be candid and honest with me. She affirmed that she had worked at the company for eight years and that Dave had been her boss the entire time. I asked her if Dave had ever approached her and asked for sexual favors. She smiled, almost smirked, and told me that after about six months, maybe a little less or more, he approached her, put his arm around her, basically bracing her so that she couldn't move and had asked for oral sex. How did she respond? She told me that she looked up into his eyes and began to smile as if she liked the idea. When he relaxed his grip around her, she reached down, grabbed him by his crotch, and twisted and squeezed until he dropped in pain to his knees. While maintaining a vice-like grip, she told him that if he ever said anything like that to her again, she knew how, and would proceed to, kill him with electricity. Clear enough? He never approached her or asked for sexual favors again. I asked her if she knew if he had asked Abby for sexual favors, and she said she suspected so but that it was not her business.

I then spoke with several of the men on the work crew to see if they had known anything about a relationship between Dave and Abby. They denied having any knowledge of any activity between the two and were basically uncooperative. However, they did ask why this was such a big deal. They said rough sex talk had occurred on the construction sites for years, and they liked it under the old president, when they could say anything and act like real men. Apparently, they had now been told they would have to "baby" the women crew members and "behave" themselves around them.

When I met with Ryan, I told him to get his checkbook ready and suggested that perhaps he should just hand over the company keys to this victim because I believed that I had substantiated the allegations. There was no excuse, no argument that could be made, and no defense that could be launched by the company to get out from under this one. It was probably going to be a multi-million dollar expense. The DOL and OSHA would probably come down on the company with seven-figure fines, and the victim could probably expect a multi-million dollar restitution. Ryan asked why I thought the outcome would be so dire and so expensive. I told them that since the company had a long history of sexist and chauvinistic behavior, his father and many of the workers on the crew would make very easy targets for the lawyers on the other side. Abby had actually met the definition of providing the company notice when she spoke to the engineer over a year ago. Unfortunately, the way she provided notice was so obtuse that it went right over the engineer's head. Be that as it may, obtuse or not, it would still qualify for notice. The company underreacted. In actuality, they failed to react at all, and the government's agencies and media would have a field day at the company's expense. Even given that Abby would make a poor witness, I felt certain she would prevail.

Young Ryan rightfully saw his company and his future going down the drain. He asked me to talk to her and do something, actually anything, to fix it and I told him I would try. The first thing we needed to do was to terminate Dave. Ryan started to protest because Dave was important to the company; he was supervising multiple construction projects and crews. I told the young president that if he underreacted at this point, he would be unequivocally sealing his fate. He had to demonstrate to OSHA, the labor department, and potentially the courts, that since he became fully aware of the severity of the situation, he was taking definitive, precipitous action. I told him that if he did not terminate Dave, and he somehow sidestepped Abby and any other allegations or victims appeared, there would be no stopping the resulting litigation. Dave was a sexual predator, and he had to be separated from the company. The company could not sue him, only Abby could. I told Ryan that he had to do everything within his control to send the message that he supported the victim and abhorred what had happened on his watch.

Ryan agreed, and I proceeded to terminate Dave. He was informed that he could be criminally prosecuted for sexual battery and that the company was ready for anything he thought he could throw at them. There was no severance, there was no deal, and he was "perp-walked" from the premises. Once he understood what he was facing, he actually went fairly quietly and was never heard from again.

I then began a series of conversations with Abby to get to know her and figure out what made her tick. She turned out to be a very weak and timid person who looked and acted like a victim. No wonder Dave had targeted her. Her persona was diametrically opposite of Jill's. As I got to know her, I learned that she had a failed dream of becoming an engineer. When asked why she gave up on that dream, she laughed a sad laugh and gave me the usual excuses of being too old, not having enough money, and no one else in her family having ever gone to college.

Letting Abby know that she was eligible for a paid leave of absence, I told her that she might be selling herself short and should take placement and aptitude tests, see what the results showed, and take time to figure out her best course of action regarding her future. I was actually a little bit ahead of myself because Ryan had not authorized any paid leave of absence, but this woman needed to be away from the company for her own protection. I had no doubt this qualified under "do anything" to fix it.

Next, I approached Ryan and told him that I was formulating a plan that was clearly a long shot but one that just might save his company's soul and financial future. He threw up his hands and again told me to do whatever was necessary to save his company. Fix the mess.

Going back to Abby, I told her that she was on a paid leave of absence now and also for the foreseeable future. We talked about what the ideal work-related future would be from her perspective, and she expressed a desire to be a mechanical engineer. Following my suggestion, she went to a career guidance center, took the exam, blew the top off of it, and discovered she had a real aptitude for the math. With her test score in hand, I asked her where she'd like to go to college. She identified the school, and I offered to go talk to the dean of the engineering program with her. Her eyes got real wide, and she asked if I knew him. I told her no, but I knew he would see us. At the appointment, I told the dean that this person was very special to our company. If he would accept her into his program, our company would pay the full tuition, in addition to books and any other assistance she might need. My request was for him to shepherd her through the program. He assured us that he would give the matter his full consideration and get back to us shortly. With her high test scores, her high school transcripts, and the promise of a fully funded student, it was an easy decision to accept her. All he had to do was look after her a bit as her age made her a non-traditional student.

Once we got her acceptance letter, I talked to her about a contract with the construction firm. I spoke with Ryan and told him I thought she would be willing to resign and sign a hold harmless waiver if he were to agree to cover her school expenses and a small living stipend. We estimated the cost and he agreed. Going back to Abby, I told her that her previous employer would agree to pay her tuition, books, and perhaps a stipend of $250 a month for the full term of her bachelors degree. All she had to do was resign and sign a waiver promising not to take any action against the construction company now or anytime in the future. She was thrilled and signed immediately. The whole deal, including my fee, cost the construction company less than $400,000.

When I tell this story, people say, "Oh great, you raped her again!" She could have received millions, and you got her to settle for less than $400,000. The truth of the matter is that this was a fabulous deal for both parties. Not in a million years would the victim have been able to stand up to the legal fight that would have occurred. In my opinion, she probably would not have been able to withstand the pressure of the depositions, let alone cross-examinations. The battle would have, or could have, lasted for years, and while I'm sure she would have eventually prevailed, the toll on her would have been enormous. This way, she was able to spend her time and efforts building a future rather than arguing about the past. Of course, the construction company got away cheap, but $400,000 isn't peanuts either. This case ended positively. The dean of the engineering school did help her through the maze of higher education, and Abby called me regularly over the course of her education. She is now an engineer.

Comparing the two cases, both women clearly had very different thresholds. The married, Pakistani woman saw sex and illicit intention where there was none. The plumber's assistant tolerated sexual battery in the workplace. What happened to Abby flies in the face of everything that is good, just, and appropriate in the workplace; she was a victim in a terrible nightmare. The lesson here is that powerful people, people like the superintendent, do not value timidity in any form. They don't value timid people, they don't value timid behavior, and once they find a doormat, they will wipe their feet on it over and over and over again. Remember Jill, the electrician's helper? She was the opposite of a doormat. Powerful and threatening, she was effective in dissuading Dave from ever approaching her for sex again. Abby always appeared, and indeed acted, weak. She begged, she cried, and in the end she was victimized.

Business owners need to create a legal and safe environment for their employees. The old president of the construction company failed in every arena. Ryan, his son, took steps to make things right both for the immediate victim and to make sure that there would be no future victims. The courts, the state and federal human rights commissions, and the court of public opinion would have rolled over and probably destroyed that company had Ryan not taken the actions he did.

Management Lessons

1. One thing that stood out in this case was the cultural difference between people. The Pakistani woman in the first case clearly viewed the situation (being invited to lunch) through the "eyes" or prism of her culture. We are now who we were then. We all have different thresholds resulting from our upbringing. These cultural differences exist separately and apart from the laws and rules that apply in the business setting. Even though the Pakistani woman felt she was the victim of sexual harassment, in the eyes of the arbitrator she was not. Clearly in that case there was a winner and a loser. It would've been better if a win/win situation could have been developed. This case had to go to an arbitrator due to the self-report component, but whenever possible, mediation is a better solution to problems because it puts the authority to decide in the hands of the disputants, and it allows for facilitation instead of arbitration.

2. The determination of the presence of sexual harassment in 90% of the cases that occur is based upon the question, "Would a reasonable woman find *that* behavior offensive?" The answer is not always easy to conclude. There is also the question of retaliation. The DOL is very sensitive to this notion, and their position is very

clear. The employer will not allow any action to be taken against the whistleblower, the person alleging that they have been the victim of sexual harassment. If any adverse action is taken against the whistleblower, a charge of retaliation can be asserted. While it may be difficult to assert that sexual harassment has occurred and sustain that position, it is relatively easy to assert and sustain a charge of retaliation. Once an employer gets tagged with a charge of retaliation, the fines and penalties really start adding up.

3. I also referred to the state and federal human rights commissions in this case. Every state has a human rights commission that is tasked with investigating charges made by employees against their employers in fairness related matters. The federal government has its own human rights commission that is called the Equal Employment Opportunity Commission (the EEOC). These are organizations set up by the government to provide the opportunity for individual employees to seek redress from transgressions made against them by their employers. These bodies have the legal authority to investigate, to arbitrate, and to fine the employer if they find the employer to be guilty of violating the employee's rights or the DOL's regulations. The fines are usually set at three times actual damages.

    For example, an employee reports that he or she has not received overtime compensation for hours worked. Let's say that the employee asserts that his or her employer has failed to pay them $2000 in overtime compensation. The EEOC or the state human rights commission will take the report, and if they think it's credible, they will conduct an investigation. They will not limit their investigation to look just at that particular employee but will look at all employees' timecards. Their assertion or position is that if the employer would do this with one person, they could do it with other employees. Let's say they identify 20 employees that did not receive their overtime. The investigating agency will now require the employer to pay the $2000 in overtime compensation to the first person, the whistleblower, but also the full compensation to the other 20 employees also identified. For the sake of this example, let's say each of the other 20 were also owed $2000 in overtime compensation. The employer now has an obligation to pay $2000 to each of the 21 employees which adds up to $42,000. The fine is usually set at three times actual damage, so the fine will be $126,000 paid to the investigating agency. The investigating agency will also issue a "right to sue letter." This document can then be taken to any lawyer who will file a civil lawsuit against the employer. Now the employer has hundreds of thousands of dollars in legal fees and court costs with which to contend. The message that the agencies, whether state or federal, wish to convey is "Don't mess with your employees!" And, it's a powerful message.

Chapter 7

Overt, Inadvertent, and Opportunistic Acts: Katrina and the Office Clown

With this case, I'm reminded of the John Mellencamp song that said, "This is a little ditty, about Jack and Diane, two American kids doing the best that they can." Well, this is a little ditty about Katrina and Brett, two American workers whose behavior put them and a company at risk. It started out pretty innocently. Katrina was in the employee lounge reading her book — that's all, just reading during a work break. There was an incident between them, and I was called in to investigate. This company was what I would describe as a pretty normal white-collar work setting. It was not a high-performance organization, just a typical software company that happened to be in the Midwest. I was called by the CEO, Carl, of this software company of about 60 people. Profitable and typical of many software companies, it was pretty casual about most things.

Before I get into the case, let me say that there are three different types of behaviors: overt, inadvertent, and opportunistic. Overt behavior is behavior on a plan. A person decides he or she is going to do something and then does it. For example, a person specifically chooses a particular outfit from a full wardrobe to work on a particular day. The underlying message from the choice might be, "I am sexy or hip or powerful etc."

That's an example of overt behavior. Another example of overt behavior is a policy that specifies that employees show up at eight o'clock ready for work. So, the employee plans his or her morning to have time to get up, get ready, and arrive just before eight o'clock. That is overt behavior, behavior on a plan.

Inadvertent behavior could be described as autopilot behavior. A good example of auto pilot behavior could be what happened when you pulled into your driveway after driving all the way home from work and realized that you couldn't remember one thing about the trip home. This is an example of autopilot behavior that undoubtedly has happened to all of us at one time to another. I'm going to guess that, on that trip, no pedestrians were hit, no traffic laws were broken, and no incidents of any kind occurred. Other examples of autopilot behavior are that jokesters tell jokes, smokers light up at specific times or places, and bodybuilders go to the gym. On a more serious note, insensitive people use racist or sexist terminology in their everyday speech. They don't think about these things because they just do them routinely. Another example could be dressing in sloppy or comfortable clothes without thinking that they may not be appropriate when a formal workday has been planned. Inadvertent behavior is behavior that occurs without people thinking. People who are "touchy-feely" types touch other people without thinking; they just do it.

The third kind of behavior is opportunistic and could even be described as predatory behavior. With this kind of behavior, the individual sees an opportunity to take advantage of a person or a situation and then does so. There are a lot of examples of opportunistic or predatory behavior in the workplace. There was an example in the news a few years ago involving Southwest Airlines. Famous for their flight attendants' antics, most people enjoy the departure from the formal airline recitation. A flight attendant, in an attempt to get the passengers to take their seats so the plane could take off, picked up the microphone and said, "Eeny, meany, miny, mo, take your seats; it's time to go." Two African-American passengers somehow became offended and filed a lawsuit against the airline and the flight attendant alleging racial insensitivity. Since the flight attendant and her supervisor were under the age of 30, they were completely unaware that in the 1950's there was a racial slur that went like this: "Eeny, meany, miny, mo, catch a "N word" by the toe." The African-American passengers threatened to file legal action against the airline in an attempt to extract a settlement.

Another example of opportunistic behavior occurs during employment interviews. It typically looks like this: The person being interviewed offers, or provides illegal information such as the number of children she has. Sometime in the interview, she might mention that she is a single mom with four children under the age of five. To see how this would be opportunistic, a little background might be helpful. Under the rules of the DOL, questions such as "Are you married? Do you have children? I noticed you have a big scar on your right hand; how did that happen?" are all illegal because they are not job related. The question, "How many kids do you have?" is irrelevant to the person's ability or candidacy for the job. The DOL has stipulated that any question that is not directly related to the job is impermissible, and if the interviewer asked such questions and/or factors the answers into their hiring decisions, they have broken the rules. and can be held legally accountable. As a practical matter, the employer might see them as relevant in that if a candidate has several young children, the employer knows that the kids could potentially have a significant impact on his or her reliability and attendance, especially in a single parent situation. That candidate could be expected to miss work due to childcare responsibilities. Even though the prospective employer may consider this kind of information relevant, the DOL sees the information as discriminatory and forbids it being factored into the hiring decision.

Continuing along this line, the first few minutes of most employment interviews are typically the "warm-up" period, and most inexperienced interviewers use this time to "warm up" themselves as well as the person being interviewed. This period is the equivalent to the question "How are you today?" It is a salutation that is factored into almost every encounter between people. Ninety-nine times out of 100 times, this question is asked with no real interest in the answer —it's a greeting, not a real question. Under the rules of the DOL, the entire time spent between the interviewer and the interviewee constitutes the interview, and during an interview, only lawful or permissible questions can be asked. This warm-up period, for most inexperienced interviewers is the autopilot portion of the interview and is often the "breeding ground" for opportunistic behavior. The following example of this behavior has happened thousands of times. Sometimes, it is the inexperienced interviewers and sometimes, more often than you might think, it is the opportunistic interviewees who provide information that is not asked for but gets factored into the interview. If it gets factored into the interview, it can be asserted that the information was factored into the hiring decision. If the interviewer is a note taker, and if the interviewee can get the interviewer to make a note when illegal information is provided, then the interviewee has just gained a huge advantage.

Let's say that the interviewee does not get the job offer. The interviewee can allege or assert that she did not get the job because she had been discriminated against due to her status as a single mom with four kids under the age of five. Ouch. The interviewer can assert, until "the cows come home" that the candidate's status as a single mom with kids never entered into the decision of whether she was selected or not selected for the position. The opportunistic interviewee or their legal counsel will assert that it was important enough to be notated, so it must've been important enough to be factored into the decision. Gotcha. This sort of assertion is worth a $7-$10,000 settlement to avoid a nuisance suit. I have known individuals that pull this stunt four to five times a year on inexperienced interviewers. It's a pretty good living when you stop to think about it. This is opportunistic behavior in its most glaring light.

To review, there are three types of behavior out there: overt which is planned behavior; inadvertent which is autopilot behavior, and opportunistic or predatory behavior. Whenever autopilot behavior collides with inadvertent behavior, inadvertent behavior will always be trashed. So someone who asserts that they're offended by racial comments will inevitably call out the person that inadvertently uses sexist or racist language at work. The offended person can assert that they've actually been assaulted by the language or terminology, and now there is a race-based discrimination case percolating. The person who originally used the inappropriate and insensitive language can claim, all day long, that they didn't mean anything by what they said. Too bad. Whether the behavior was autopilot or overt, the damage has still been done and liability has been exposed. Sometimes the solution is a monetary settlement, and sometimes the solution is someone gets fired.

In this case, Carl was in his office with the door closed working away. It was the old cliché, "I was minding my own business when ..." The door flew open and the employee, whom he recognized as Katrina, an accountant from the business office, ran into his office and literally screamed at him to give her his suit coat. Carl noticed that Katrina's silk blouse was wet exposing her very ample chest. He immediately took off his suit coat, gave it to her, and she used it to cover herself up. Katrina was so emotional that she was literally beside herself. He tried to get her to calm down and explain what happened but Katrina could do neither. Aware that she was too emotional to even explain herself, she blurted out that she was going home, turned around, and left the office. The whole encounter ended as abruptly as it had started. Carl realized that his car keys were in his coat pocket and now he was stranded at work. Great. His only consolation was that his billfold, which was usually in the breast pocket, today was in his pant's pocket, so he at least had that! Carl's day had certainly been interrupted by this incident, and he then attempted to figure out not only what had happened but also what had precipitated it. He started with Katrina's immediate supervisor, the company's CFO, George

He called George and asked him to come to his office. After relaying the story, he asked if George could shed any light on any aspect of it. George was unaware of the actual incident, but shared that Katrina was a very attractive woman who was private, not particularly friendly, and perhaps a bit strange. She had been with the company approximately a year and was meticulous about every aspect of her work. George didn't really know much about her because she kept to herself, but he did respect her. She was always on time, dressed impeccably, and always produced competent and accurate work. The only thing that George would ask for would be for her to be a bit friendlier and more a part of the team. That was all he could offer.

A little later in the day, an employee, Brett, knocked on Carl's door and asked for a few minutes. Carl invited him to enter and asked what was on his mind. Brett had a concerned, albeit sheepish, look on his face. He acknowledged that he had been involved in an incident that had occurred in the employee lounge about an hour earlier. Brett said that he had gone into the employee lounge earlier that day and found it empty, except for Katrina who had been sitting over in the corner reading a book. He now had Carl's full attention. Brett said hello to Katrina, but she ignored him. He repeated his greeting and, again, received no response.

He told Carl that he had a quart-sized water bottle in his hand, the kind that did not have a screw on top, but rather a push-pull nipple as its cap. Carl was familiar with this type of water container. One simply pulled on the nipple and that opened the container so that water could either be squeezed or sucked out, then pushed close between drinks. Wondering about the relevance of this, Carl encouraged Brett to continue, which he did willingly. He indicated that he walked up to Katrina, and while standing in front of her, said hello for the third time. And, for the third time, she ignored him so he decided he was going to squeeze a drop of water from this container on to the book to get her attention. As luck and Murphy's Law will always attest, just as he attempted to dribble a drop of water, the nipple on the bottle came loose and the full contents came splashing out. The water hit the book and cascaded onto Katrina's silk blouse, soaking it, and therefore exposing her chest. For Brett, dripping the water on Katrina's book was autopilot behavior, true to his nature of harmless, somewhat impulsive acts. He was not overtly trying to upset or harass her; it was an unpredictable chain of events.

Katrina jumped up, obviously surprised, and immediately recognized that she was exposed so she ran out of the lounge and down the hall. It happened so quickly, Brett did not get a chance to apologize, say, or do anything; Katrina just disappeared. He reiterated that it had been an accident and that there had been no intention to harm or hurt her. He just thought he would get her attention by dribbling a drop of water on her book to break her concentration and allow her to recognize his presence. Brett said he'd been drinking out of the bottle for the better part of the morning and did not know that the top was loose. Carl told Brett to return to work, and he would get back with him as quickly as possible.

Carl knew me, called, and asked if I was available to come over immediately and assist him in dealing with this situation. Not enough was known about Katrina's personality or proclivities to make an immediate determination regarding whether she might sue or how she would respond to the situation. She had been exposed, and humiliated, at least she thought so. At the very least, she had been highly excited. Carl didn't feel equipped to address the situation further. When I arrived, he told me the situation, and I asked for 30 minutes to prepare a proposal. I assured him that my scope documents would not take much time and would provide the clarity I felt would be useful prior to interceding. I drafted my usual documents, and he reviewed and accepted them so I could begin my investigation.

Since Katrina had vacated the premises in a highly emotional state, I couldn't go with my usual rule of interviewing the victim first. I decided to gather as much background information as might be available on site. My first stop was a meeting with George, Katrina's immediate supervisor. He gave me the same information he had provided to Carl. It wasn't much to go on, but it was what it was. My next interview was with Brett's immediate supervisor. I found out that Brett had been with the company for almost five years. He did solid work, everybody liked him, and he was a bit of a jokester. His antics at work were harmless, elevated morale, and appeared to everyone to be "in good fun." There was nothing mean-spirited or harmful in his behavior over the course of his employment. Interesting.

I then interviewed Brett who exhibited honest contrition. He assured me that there had been no intention to embarrass or harm Katrina in any way. Brett did not think she was trying to ignore him, but rather she appeared so deep in concentration that she simply didn't notice him. His attempt to gain her acknowledgment had gone badly astray. He was sorry and wanted to say so but simply didn't get the opportunity because she ran from the room so abruptly, which he understood. Brett told me that there was no one else in the employee lounge who could act as a witness to the incident. I asked Brett if he knew Katrina and if he liked her. He said he had seen her around but didn't really know her. She never participated in or attended any of the company events or parties. He thought she was very attractive, was hoping to get to know her, and acknowledged that this incident probably ruined any chance to do so. Asking Brett if he had discussed this incident with any of his coworkers or his supervisor, it appeared that he had spoken with the supervisor but none of his coworkers, and he had no intention of discussing the matter further. I instructed him to return to work, and follow his intuition that this matter needed to remain confidential and away from the office grapevine.

My next meeting was back with Carl. I told him my findings suggested that the incident seemed harmless, an innocent accident that had gone badly. I didn't think that Brett had any malicious intent, but that until we talked to Katrina, I was at a bit of an impasse.

Carl suggested that he call Katrina ostensibly to make sure she got home okay but also to talk to her about "next steps." I agreed. Katrina answered the call, assured him that she had gotten home safely, and thanked him for the use of his coat. Carl told her that the HR consultant had been called in to assist in addressing the situation. By this time it was 3:30 in the afternoon, and there was no point in suggesting she return to work. When he asked her about coming to work the next day, she said she was planning on it. He advised her that her first meeting would be with the HR consultant, this guy named Steve. He said he would see her in the morning and reminded her to bring back his coat.

Katrina and I arrived about the same time, Carl introduced us, and then left us staring at each other in the privacy of his office. I reintroduced myself, provided some background information, and asked her to take me through the incident. Katrina held her head high, had perfect posture, and looked completely put together. Every hair was in place, her manicure was perfect, and her clothes were feminine and tasteful. She explained that she had been in the break room, minding her own business and reading a book as it was her favorite stress reliever and she read during most of her breaks. Saying she had a right to do that during her breaks, Katrina said she did nothing to incite or invite any attention from anyone. Her words were clipped, as was her demeanor.

I asked about her concentration when she was reading. She told me it was deep and that she often set a small alarm so that she would not overshoot her break period. Then I asked her about her experiences at work, if she liked her job, her coworkers or her supervisor. With a puzzled look, she commented that she liked her work as an accountant, found her supervisor to be competent and knowledgeable, and didn't really know, or care to know, any of her coworkers. She made it a rule not to fraternize or socialize with coworkers. I asked her if she knew Brett, the person who splashed water on her the previous day. She assumed a condescending posture and tone and advised that she had seen him around, but did not know him or even his name. Again, she emphasized her rule not to associate with coworkers.

Changing tactics, the next question was about how she felt about the incident. Indignant, she asked me how I would feel if I were startled out of my concentration only to discover that I was wet and exposed. She was red-faced, which I interpreted as something between embarrassment and anger. I said I understood and before I could ask her what she would like to see happen, she said that she thought that Brett should be terminated for what he had done. Did she think he had humiliated her and embarrassed her on purpose? Her response to this was, "What does that matter?" I said that I thought it mattered a lot. If he did it on purpose, there was been malice of forethought, but if he did it accidentally, then there was no malice intended. She hesitated and obviously thought it through but concluded that she was a completely innocent victim who was personally and intimately impacted by Brett's behavior. She said the incident might constitute sexual harassment. The consequences of such actions, in her mind, should be serious. I told her that she was obviously a very serious person, probably a very careful person, and that I had guessed she never engaged in horseplay. She acknowledged that I was correct and insightful. When asked if she really thought about it, deeply, if she would really want to see Brett fired over the incident, she said yes, but that she recognized it was not up to her. Now I was wondering if this was opportunistic behavior, building to a possible lawsuit. Not knowing Katrina, it was impossible to tell at this point.

I explained that the definition of sexual harassment was unwelcome, unsolicited, and unreciprocated behavior of a sexual nature and that the criterion for determining sexual harassment was built around the question, "Would a reasonable woman find the behavior offensive?" I also told her that sexual harassment manifested itself in one of three ways: quid pro quo (which I explained), sexual harassment through sexual favoritism, and sexual harassment through hostile work environment, which had to occur in a pattern. If it occurred as an isolated incident, it may be inappropriate, but it was not sexual harassment. She asked me if I felt quite smug about this. I told her no, that I was just trying to provide her with insight and accurate information.

Telling her I would get back to her soon and advise her of my findings and conclusions, I suggested that she return to work as if nothing had happened. I assured her that my work the previous day protected her confidentiality and that this matter had not been, nor would be, the subject of gossip and idle conversation. The company, despite Brett's behavior, was a professional place, and the matter would be handled in a professional manner.

I returned to Carl's office and asked if he would be comfortable calling a meeting with George and Brett's immediate supervisor. He agreed and called the two into his office for an impromptu meeting. I provided my findings and drew the conclusion that Brett's behavior amounted to harmless, but nevertheless, inappropriate horseplay. Horseplay inevitably results in negative unintended consequences I pontificated. Someone gets hurt, something gets broken, productivity suffers, and professionalism takes a hit. That's exactly what happened here. I asked if anyone disagreed, and no one did. I believed that, while Brett was well liked and had a good work record, he also had a reputation of being kind of a joker. Katrina, on the other hand, was not well liked but was well respected by her supervisor. She had the right to be where she was and doing what she was doing. Brett had no right to take the action that he took. While there was no foul intended, there was foul play experienced by Katrina.

I told the group that I thought that terminating Brett was unnecessary and represented "overkill" even though Katrina solicited it. Brett should receive a written reprimand to be placed in his permanent personnel file and also be required to provide Katrina a written, not oral, not face-to-face, but written note of apology. I suggested that the apology be conveyed through George instead of directly to Katrina from Brett. He should also pay the laundry bill for Katrina's blouse. I assumed it was not ruined because it was only doused with water, but if it was ruined, then Brett or the company should replace it. Brett should be told that should any other incident arise out of his proclivity toward horseplay, termination could result. Regarding Katrina, I thought it would be a shame if she were to voluntarily quit because the company chose not to terminate Brett. I suggested that her immediate supervisor, George, and I could meet with her an attempt to end this matter in a way that might bring closure that she could accept. Again, even though we didn't know if Katrina would exhibit opportunistic behavior, we had to act on the possibility. Based on my experience, this was definitely a situation that fit the adage of better safe than sorry.

Brett's supervisor indicated his comfort in addressing the reprimand with Brett directly. He acknowledged that he appreciated my participation in attempting to close the matter with Katrina and that he did not want to lose her as a result of this incident. Carl agreed and asked me to report back after the meeting with Katrina.

Fortunately, when George and I went into Katrina's office, we discovered it was private so we did not attract unwanted attention. When we were all seated, I told her that I had concluded my investigation and provided my recommendations to her immediate supervisor and Carl. I said that I thought the incident was an unfortunate accident that amounted to horseplay, and the company was officially sorry and wished to state that formally. She was told that Brett was also sorry and would be providing a written apology that she could expect within the day. Katrina said the blouse was not ruined, and I told her the company would take care of the bill. Reminding her that she had the company's and Carl's personal apology for the ordeal, I hoped she could accept this as the company's sincere response.

Then Katrina asked if the company was going to terminate Brett. I told her no. She asked what would happen to him, and I told her that it was a confidential personnel matter and that it would be inappropriate for me to say. I assured her that the matter was being taken care of and asked for her understanding and professionalism, restating that the company took the matter seriously and intended to handle it. She was to feel free to report any incident in which she felt uncomfortable to her supervisor and that the company valued her, and valued her safety and comfort. With all my conviction, I said that I hoped she would be satisfied that the company responded appropriately. As important as it is to try to ward off any opportunistic behavior in a situation like this, it is just as important to remain cognizant of the individual's perspective. There was also the possibility that Katrina was truly upset and humiliated by the experience, and it was her way of reacting to it, as opposed to pursuing a lawsuit.

I invited George to come in and personally assure her that he too, hoped that she would be satisfied with this outcome and could put the matter behind her. He communicated sincerely and warmly, yet professionally. We exited her office with the matter of her "next steps" or her response still remaining ambiguous.

After we were back in George's office, I asked him what he thought she would do. He really did not know but felt confident that we had done everything we could and treated her with respect and courtesy. He thanked me and told me that he learned a lot from the experience. I returned to Carl's office, gave him a report, and asked him to keep me apprised if Katrina walked out. He told me that accounting was a fungible skill, and if Katrina needed to be replaced, she could be. Thanking me, he told me that he appreciated how the case was handled. He added that he thought it was a little ironic that Katrina, as the accounts payable accountant, would be cutting my check. I suggested that he was right and that I hoped that the act of cutting my check would have no effect on her feelings whatsoever.

The case ended with Brett learning the consequences of his thoughtlessness. He wrote a sincere apology and paid the laundry bill for the silk blouse. A written reprimand now blemished an otherwise spotless record. He also perceived that he lost any chance to get to know or date Katrina who evidently accepted that Brett was not going to be terminated, and she remained on the job. She confirmed a notion that I have had for quite some time: healthy people have to have their say; unhealthy people have to have their way.

In this case, if Katrina had been opportunistic or predatory, she could have pressed her point and sought a remedy very different than what actually happened. She could have threatened or filed a sexual harassment case against the company. The result would've been that the company would have negotiated her exit with a signed, hold harmless waiver in exchange for a payment that might have been in the $25,000 range. She might've lost her position, but with her looks and education, she would have had no trouble securing another job. She was neither opportunistic nor predatory, but rather overt in her behavior. Brett had exhibited autopilot behavior that collided with Katrina's overt behavior. The result was Brett was reprimanded, and Katrina got the apology. The company got away cheap, but lessons were learned all the way around.

Management Lessons

1. There are three types of behaviors: overt behavior (behavior on a plan), inadvertent behavior (autopilot behavior), and opportunistic (predatory) behavior. Most people operate using autopilot behavior. They do things without really thinking about them first simply because that's what they normally do in a given situation. For example, some people engage in gossip and storytelling about other people. They don't stop to consider whether it's appropriate or inappropriate; they just do it because that's what they do. Another example might be joke telling. There are those who like telling jokes and enjoy hearing them, but jokes are often racist, sexist, or judgmental with somebody being the brunt of the joke. People on autopilot don't think about whether it's appropriate or inappropriate to tell jokes at work; they just do it.

Overt behavior is behavior on a plan. Overt would be: I'm in a work related situation so I shouldn't "let my hair down" and do something or say something that could get me in trouble or threaten my job. If I were a person who enjoyed telling jokes, but realized that telling jokes in a workplace situation could be inappropriate, I would refrain from doing so. When I do that, I am practicing overt behavior. Overt behavior is behavior that is specifically chosen. Even a clothing choice can be overt behavior. For example, a person who is most comfortable in jeans chooses to wear business attire for a meeting. That choice is overt behavior. The same person on autopilot would have worn the jeans, not thinking about the appropriate clothing for the situation.

The third kind of behavior is opportunistic or even predatory behavior. This is behavior that is also overt, but it's a different kind of overt. With opportunistic behavior, a person chooses to use a situation to his or her advantage. For example, I overhear two employees telling off-color jokes to each other, clearly inappropriate to the work setting. While I am not particularly offended by the jokes, I wish to get one of the two employees in trouble. I take advantage of the opportunity and complain to the supervisor that I was offended by the sexist or racist subject matter I overheard. Knowing that sexist or racist subject matter has no place in the workplace, I chose to take steps to get the other person in trouble, perhaps even fired. That's opportunistic behavior. I wasn't really offended, but I took the opportunity to use the situation to my advantage.

Whenever there is a collision between opportunistic behavior and inadvertent behavior, the person operating on autopilot will generally be subordinated. Using the example above, there is no legitimate defense for telling inappropriate jokes at work. The offended person's position will be the position honored or supported by management. Management cannot say to the offended person, "Just forget it and get over it." Their position must be to support the offended person even if the offended person made a false claim.

Management must assume that the offended person was truly offended. There is clearly opportunistic or predatory behavior in this situation.

The answer is to not "let your hair down" at work. All choices and all behavior should be appropriate to the setting. Because there are rules at work that are more stringent than the rules that apply outside of work, it stands to reason that behavior at work should be at all times justifiable. Most overt choices (behaviors) are more explainable and justifiable than inadvertent or autopilot behaviors.

2. During job interviews, there are legal as well as illegal questions. It is illegal to ask questions that are not related to the job. Some questions are innocent ones but could still be illegal. An example could be: I, as the interviewer, notice that you (the interviewee) are wearing a wedding band. I then ask the question, "Are you married?" This is an illegal question. Whether or not a candidate is married is irrelevant and immaterial to the job. Only questions that are directly relevant and material to the job can be asked during an interview. If the interviewer asks the candidate illegal questions, the candidate can hold the interviewer and the company accountable for asking questions that are illegal. This could be an opportunity for predatory opportunistic behavior. The interviewer needs to operate overtly and prepare specific, job-related questions for the candidates to answer.

This is an important point. Interview situations are highly sensitive situations that create far more liability for the interviewer then for the interviewee. The interviewer might ask, "Have you ever had a workers' comp. claim?" This may be relevant or important information to the interviewer, but it is also highly illegal because it is irrelevant to the current prospective job. Let's say the candidate answered the question. "Yes, I have had a workers' comp. claim in the past." If the candidate did not get the position, the candidate could say he or she was rejected because of the information he or she provided during the interview. The candidate could file a complaint with the EEOC or the state human rights commission claiming discrimination by the prospective employer or because they filed a workers comp claim in the past. That prospective employer would have no defense and would be fined as well as owe some sort of compensation or restitution to the candidate for the discrimination.

Chapter 8

Counseling vs. Termination: Two Who Almost Crossed the Line

Terminating an employee should be considered only after specific steps have been taken to correct the situation that is causing the termination to be discussed. This chapter will provide several examples of the use of counseling as a method for redirecting non-performing employees, therefore rehabilitating their status within their company.

The law follows baseball's three strikes rule. If an employee is not performing, the DOL expects the employer to advise that employee regarding the problem, tell him or her how to fix it, document it, and provide a reasonable amount of time to demonstrate that corrective action has occurred. If this has occurred and the employee is still not performing, the law expects the supervisor to try again. By law, the supervisor is expected to again tell the employee what is wrong, how to fix it, document it, and give time to demonstrate that it has been fixed. If, after this second attempt, the employee continues to fail, the employer is within his or her rights to terminate the employee. That termination should prevail and be upheld even if the terminated employee exercises his or her recourse options and files action against the employer.

The corrective action and documentation piece is a very important part of the equation, and it is called due process. The first time the supervisor addresses a matter with the employee is called an oral warning. Under the law, an oral warning is not considered discipline. It does not need to be written down (documented) and/or formally placed in the employee's permanent record. If the employee satisfactorily corrects the matter, the matter is closed and that is that—work life goes on.

If the employee has not successfully corrected the matter and the supervisor chooses to revisit it, the employer is now entering or engaging in disciplinary action. At this step in the process, there is a need to document the situation or matter in the employee's permanent file. If it is not documented, then as far as the DOL is concerned, it did not happen. This is called a written warning and is the first formal step of discipline in the corrective action process. The longer, more appropriate way to describe this is that it is a written documentation of a written warning. Sounds redundant, but it can't be stressed enough that there needs to be a written record of a written warning. When the supervisor enters this stage, there is a need to go back and document the oral warning as well. This is called a written documentation of the oral warning. It is permissible, in fact necessary under the law, to draft this document ex post facto, after-the-fact. Remember, if the situation is fixed, there is no need to document it, but if it's not fixed over the passage of time, seeing the reoccurring "bad" or incorrect behavior needs to be readdressed by the supervisor. So now, the supervisor has two documents to draft. One is the written documentation of a written warning (written in present tense), and the next is the ex post facto written documentation. The written documentation of the oral warning is in past tense and documents the counseling session that occurred in the previous weeks or months when the matter was first addressed. The written documentation of the written warning is in present tense documenting what the supervisor is doing presently in an attempt to correct the matter.

The format for each of these documents will be highlighted shortly. Now, let's get into a case which will provide a concrete example. An employee, Josh, worked in a large multi-departmental organization. The organization occupied a rather large campus containing over five different buildings. Josh worked in one department and was attracted to a female employee,

Doris, who worked in a different department in a different building. Josh's job legitimately required him to migrate to Doris's building from time to time, and he regularly took the opportunity to visit her. As these visits became more frequent, Doris took note and became annoyed. She did not seek his attention, nor did she reciprocate the attention or particularly welcome it. Does any of this have a familiar ring? It should, as it is starting to meet the definition of sexual harassment. At this point, however, the behavior is not of a sexual nature so it could be defined as harassment. It began to cross the line when Josh found out that Doris was celebrating her birthday. He bought her a small gift, and after presenting it to her, attempted to give her a hug and kiss. She realized what he was doing, did not approve, and turned her head to the side. All Josh got for his effort was a kiss full of hair. The awkward moment ended, Josh left, and Doris reported the incident to her supervisor. Doris's supervisor reported the incident to his supervisor, the department director, and I got called in to conduct a preliminary investigation and determine exactly what had happened.

I received my overview from the department director and then proceeded to interview Doris. She not only told me what had happened, but that the contacts initiated by Josh had become more frequent in the last few months. At first, she just saw him as someone from work, but as it progressed, she sensed his intentions growing toward something more personal and perhaps intimate. This was attention that she did not want. I asked her if she felt threatened or merely annoyed by Josh's overtures. At this point, I asked her to make a distinction for me and clarify if she was making a formal complaint against Josh or voicing a concern. The distinction is subtle, but very important, and a valuable tool for management. If she is voicing a concern, she can enjoy some political cover. If she is making a complaint, the matter becomes more formal and a bit more public. Doris said that she was simply voicing a concern and that what she felt at this point was annoyed. She gave me several examples of Josh's visits in which he had shown up and become a time eater. Despite various subtle techniques, it was clear he wasn't getting her point. She told me she just wanted to be left alone so she could do her job unimpeded and uninterrupted. There was no interest in a relationship of any kind with him.

My next stop was to interview Josh. I told him that an allegation had been made, or better stated, a concern voiced by Doris against him. He seemed a little surprised but did not become defensive. When asked about his relationship with Doris, he acknowledged that there wasn't much to it but that he was attracted to her and would like to see the relationship grow. I attempted to get Josh to articulate his vision of how he saw this relationship unfolding. Listening, I got the distinct impression that he was not fantasizing about her nor had he entered into an unhealthy realm that might lead to stalking. He seemed pretty normal and mentally healthy. Josh acknowledged that he was getting nowhere with his overtures to Doris. I told him that that was not quite true. He had made an impression on her and was actually on a path that could include Doris making a formal complaint of sexual harassment against him, resulting in probable termination of his position and a potential threat to his entire career. He was visibly shaken by the revelations and my forecast of his future and started to look sick. Telling him that I would get back to him, I urged him not to do anything that might be considered provocative and, above all, not to contact Doris. It was very important that he not take any steps that could undermine his position or standing with the company. He understood and even thanked me.

I then had a conversation with Josh's immediate supervisor and updated him regarding the incidents between Josh and Doris. He was surprised and caught a bit flat-footed, as he had been unaware of the entire situation. Regarding Josh's work record, he said that Josh was a good employee with a commendable work record spanning about two and half years. He asked me if I was going to recommend termination, as that was my reputation within the company. I told him no because Josh had not crossed the threshold into sexual harassment or even harassment. While he was on that glide path, his behavior was such that Doris had only registered a concern rather than a formal complaint. She was not feeling threatened, just annoyed.

Had Doris felt threatened, I might have concluded that Josh had gone so far that rehabilitation was not possible. Based upon what they both had said, I felt that Josh's job was salvageable. The superintendent concurred with my recommended course of action and appreciated avoiding the ordeal of a termination and replacement of the position. I told him to monitor Josh closely and report any concerns that he might have about Josh to his supervisor. There would be documentation by me in my file that could always be used in the future if required. Placing the document in Josh's personnel file would irrevocably tarnish him. What was necessary was for the supervisor to be aware of the situation and monitor Josh's future behavior. He agreed that it was the appropriate plan.

I had a brief conversation with Doris and asked if she would mind if her supervisor joined us. She didn't and when her supervisor arrived, I explained that I had had an extensive conversation with Josh who had assured me that he now understood Doris's wishes and expectations for the future. Doris was told that we took her concerns very seriously and not only did but would continue to take all steps necessary to protect her and provide an environment free from the kind of attention that she had experienced. If she experienced any unwelcome attention from Josh, or anybody else for that matter, she should report it to her supervisor immediately. I told her I thought that the incident was closed and asked her if she was satisfied. She was and thanked me although she did ask what happened to Josh. Since it was a confidential personnel matter, I told her I was not at liberty to discuss the particulars. It ended with me repeating that any concerns she might have in the future about this individual, or any other individual within the company, should be made known to her supervisor, and the company would take the appropriate action.

Another visit to Josh was next. I let him know that if his actions continued, it would probably result in Doris filing a formal complaint of sexual harassment. If that happened, he could expect probable termination and the possible disruption of his entire career. However, it appeared that he had not reached that point so if he could stop, the matter could be easily resolved. In the workplace, no means no — no matter how subtly the no is stated. He had received several subtle "no" messages from Doris, so it was time for a not so subtle "no" message from me. Asked if he could accept that and discontinue his contacts with, and overtures towards, Doris he said, "Oh yes." He read me "loud and clear." I told him I was going to speak with his supervisor about the situation and draft a written documentation of an oral warning. The documentation would not be placed in his permanent file but would be retained by me and then placed in his permanent file should another incident occur. If another incident did occur, this first incident would come out, a pattern would be demonstrated, and termination would surely result.

The format for the documentation is always the same. The first paragraph is a succinct description of "what went wrong." This is usually a three or four sentence overview. No treatise on the background or context of the situation is required. The second paragraph is an explanation of what the policy is, or what the company's expectations are, relative to the situation. This is three or four sentences and may include the actual restatement of the related policy. Sometimes, I like to include a statement of the company's values in this paragraph. This portion could even be written specifying that it is not a part of the company's values for any employee to exhibit these behaviors.

The next paragraph is a description of the plan of corrective action. This must include a timetable for the corrective action to become obvious as well as a statement of the consequences that will follow if the plan of action is not implemented. It is very important to state that "further disciplinary action up to and including termination" could result if the situation or problem is not fixed. The write-up must include the word "termination" so it is crystal clear that this action could result. I have been in front of administrative hearing officers, or the judge in a civil case, where the terminated employee has said, "I knew I was in trouble, but I didn't realize that I could lose my job over this, after all I only stole from them . . . or I only threatened to slug my boss. Does that seem like a termination offense?" The bottom line is if the employee could be terminated if the situation continued, then the write-up must specify that further disciplinary action up to and including *termination* could result.

Another little point, but an important one, is that the documentation needs to be addressed or directed to the personnel file, not to the individual. In addition, the document needs to be addressed not to the individual, but to the individual's personnel file. Let me demonstrate, using the incident between Josh and Doris. Using company letterhead, I specify the following:

At the top of the document I write: MEMO.

Line one states from whom the memo is written: Steve Cohen, personnel consultant

Line two states to whom the memo is being written: to personnel file (in this case)

Line three specifies the date the document is being written.

Line four specifies Re: written documentation of performance concerns about Josh

Once the documentation is written in this way, it is clear that the document is written to, and therefore belongs to, the personnel file. While it is being written *about* Josh, it is not being written *to* Josh. If it were written to an individual, then that individual would own it and have rights to it. By writing the document to the personnel file, it is clear that the personnel file is owned by the company. The company has fewer legal obligations and requirements in this situation than it would if the document was written to the individual. This way the document does not need to be provided to the employee, and it doesn't need to be signed by the individual. This is a subtle, but very important, point.

Going back to the case, I notified the person who hired me, the department director, that I had completed the investigation and found that there was no sexual harassment or other activities/behaviors/situations that required him to take any action. The alleged victim had not filed a formal complaint but rather had communicated a concern. Once the alleged perpetrator understood the concern and realized the potential seriousness, he was willing to change his behavior. I assured the director that through counseling everything was under control and, most importantly, all parties were satisfied. This was a good example of misbehavior caught early and redirection resulted in "no foul." I assured him that the immediate supervisors had things under control.

There were some interesting developments. About eight months later, there was a promotional opportunity within the company. Josh, now aware of appropriate work behavior, applied for the promotion and was seriously considered. As part of the interview and due diligence process, Josh's immediate supervisor was asked to provide a reference. The supervisor was, of course, aware of the situation that had occurred with Doris, and he called me regarding whether or not he should disclose the incident. I inquired if there had been any relapse on Josh's part, and he told me no. He said that Josh had veered away from Doris, and the incident had remained closed. I told him that I had suspected as much since I had not been brought back to deal with any backsliding on Josh's part. In that light, I told him that I did not feel it was appropriate to reveal the incident and to please notify me if Josh got the promotion, both of which happened.

Prior to his moving to the new position, I asked the supervisor to arrange for the three of us to meet. Josh was quite surprised and a bit concerned to see me. Most everyone is — just one of the "perks" of the job. At the meeting, I asked Josh how he felt about his new promotion, who replied that he was pleased and looking forward to it. I told Josh that his current supervisor had called me and asked if I thought the Doris situation should be revealed since he was asked for a reference. Asking Josh what he thought would have happened to his chances for the promotion had the incident been revealed, he acknowledged that his opportunity probably would have been ruined. I concurred and said that since he had agreed to "back away" from Doris and expressed contrition about the whole event, his supervisor and I had expunged the record. Since he had honored his commitment to stay away from Doris and "fly straight," we had honored him by keeping the incident confidential. We could see the sweat beginning to form on Josh's forehead. He was wondering what we wanted from him. I encouraged him to relax because there was nothing sinister going on. We just wanted him to realize that we knew he had kept his agreement and that we had honored ours. But, we expected him to remain on an honorable and professional course. We had taken a chance on him, and we wanted him to know that there was justice done at this company. His supervisor could have "played safe" and revealed the past, but he didn't. We expected Josh to continue to act professionally and become great in his new role. By doing so, he would justify the risks we had taken on his behalf.

Another case that concluded with a happy ending through counseling involved a highly paid programmer, Andrew, who had a serious tardiness problem. He was late to work at least a day or two, each and every week. His boss, the owner of a small manufacturing company had become very angry about the situation, but was so nice that he did not want to address it. The company COO had the same feelings so I was brought in to assist.

This was a sheet metal shop that employed about 85 people. The owner, Curt, was an independently wealthy person who was one of the nicest people I, personally, had ever met. The owner basically bought this business and operated it so he had something to do with his time. Curt treated the business and its employees as if they were an extension of his own family. In fact, some of the employees were his family. His son, Jackson, was the company's COO. Like all people, Curt had his limits regarding what he would tolerate.

The sheet metal shop had a variety of stamps, presses, and cutting machines. Each operator had to be highly skilled and was very well paid. It was a nonunion shop but paid union scale. There was a technical department operated by three highly paid computer programmers, and their job was to draft the technical programming specifications for each sheet metal project. These technical specifications were fed into the computers contained in the various stamps, presses, and cutting machines so that the machines could turn out a consistent product over thousands of repetitions. Consequently, these machines cost millions of dollars.

One of these programmers within the technical department was the employee in question, Andrew. He was a 39-year-old white male who was paid approximately $80,000 a year. Andrew had been employed with the company three years. In the last year and a half, his proclivity to arrive late had bloomed — and it was not a pretty flower.

Curt told me that he didn't know why Andrew had developed this tardiness pattern, but it had gotten to the point where his coworkers were complaining, and he had become more and more frustrated and angry. To start, I conducted a twelve-month time card audit on Andrew and the two other employees within the technical department. I also randomly selected half a dozen other employees and completed a time card audit on all these folks. What I discovered was that Andrew averaged two instances per week in which he arrived approximately 35 minutes late. Doing the math, that was 50 weeks x 2 incidences totaling 100 incidents. Multiplying 35 minutes times 100 incidents equaled 3,500 minutes. Taking the 3,500 minutes and dividing them by 60 gave a whopping 58.33 hours of missed time in one year. No wonder alarm bells were going off! Over the course of the previous year, two other employees within the technical department had been tardy an average of one time per month, with an average arrival time of 14 minutes late. Looking at the randomly selected half dozen employees, I discovered that their arrival times were within normal limits or expectations. The results of my audit clearly demonstrated that there was a problem with Andrew

I then reviewed the company's policy manual to see if they had a policy regarding the company's expectation about the timely arrival of all employees. Believe it or not, there was no such policy. I pointed this out to Jackson and his father, and they looked at me with incredulity. Curt asked "You mean we have to have a policy demanding that people show up for work on time?" No, I told him; you need to have a policy specifying what the official start time is for each employee.

I told them that the lowest level of organizational behavior was called a practice. For example, it is practice to show up at eight o'clock or at a specific time. It is practice to dress or to behave in a certain way. These are all practices. The next level up from the practice is a policy. It is policy to follow safety procedures, or to take our breaks at a certain time, or to require itemized receipts in order to be reimbursed for expenses. The next level up from a policy is a law or an ordinance.

The problem with operating by practices is that the courts don't recognize them as real rules. In fact, the courts have ruled on many occasions that employees can't be held legally accountable to practices, only to policies or laws or ordinances. So in effect, they both were mad at Andrew for breaking rules that didn't formally exist. I assured them that this was easy to fix by simply creating a policy. They agreed that they needed to beef up their entire policy and procedure manual to be far more comprehensive and have it upgrade the variety of practices currently in use to the level of formal policies. Before I helped them with that, however, they needed to formalize the practice of employee arrival time expectations to the level of a policy.

Following that exchange and armed with my time card audit data, I presented my findings. I told them that they were indeed correct that Andrew had a problem and that the problem was not widespread within or outside of the department. A meeting with Andrew was set for the next day. I had drafted brief scope documents articulating my objective to help Andrew understand that he was at risk of losing his job and that if he continued with the behavior, that was exactly what would happen. I specified my fee and all were in agreement. We also agreed that Curt would not be present for the session with Andrew, but that Jackson would participate.

I arrived on site the next day carrying one of my favorite props. Under my arm was a violin case. When Jackson joined me in the conference room, he immediately noticed my violin case and recognized the connotation. In the hands of a hit man, a violin case usually suggests a machine gun. Reassuring him that I carried no weapons, I opened the case to reveal a very old, broken and battered violin. The face was cracked in several places, and the strings and neck were broken. He asked me why I brought a busted up fiddle, and I told him he would find out shortly.

Andrew arrived on time that morning. What a surprise! He had been given no notice about the meeting, just invited by Jackson to come into the conference room. He arrived, saw me sitting there, and appeared totally carefree. Jackson introduced me as the company's HR consultant, we greeted each other, and I took over the conversation. I told Andrew that I had been a consultant for the company only a short period of time, but that my job was to assist Curt and Jackson with personnel matters. Asking him if he had any idea why we were meeting this morning, he replied that he had no idea but presumed I would tell him. I told him he was correct and asked him if he was aware of the time he was supposed to be at work each morning. He told me that he thought it was about eight o'clock. I told him that he was partially correct, but that it was not *about* eight o'clock, it was *actually* eight o'clock. He said, "Oh this is why we're meeting, is that right?" Letting him know he was right again, I asked if he was aware of the number of times over the course of the previous year that he had been late. He said no. Per my request to take a serious guess, he said about once a week. Then I asked him to guess how much time was associated with each one of the incidents, and he said about 15 minutes each time. Did he think anybody else in his department had a similar experience? He said that he wasn't aware his coworkers' schedules.

As for his reason for arriving late so often, Andrew said that his wife's car was not dependable and couldn't be relied upon to get her to her job every day on time. Since he didn't have to be at work on time and his wife did, he had to take her to work pretty regularly. Following up on his statement, I asked him why he felt that he didn't have to be at work on time. He shrugged his shoulders and just said, "Well, I didn't think I had to be at work on time."

It turned out that his wife was a receptionist at a $27,000 a year job. Considering this disclosure, my comment to him was "So, you're willing to put your job and $80,000 at risk to protect your wife's $27,000 year job, right?" He said that he wasn't putting his job at risk, and then it seemed to hit him. Correcting him, I clarified that he was indeed putting his $80,000 year job at risk, something he needed to understand. The proverbial light bulb slowly started to come on for Andrew. His posture changed, he sat up straight, and his facial expression became more serious. This was all good information. If he had shown contempt or a lack of interest, I would have concluded that a far more serious problem existed. Andrew was making most of the right moves, which suggested to me that the situation was salvageable, and his status could be rehabilitated.

Bringing out my findings from my time card audit, I asked him if he would be surprised to learn that it was more like two times a week that he was late, not one as he had suggested. And, would he be surprised to learn that each incident of being late racked up closer to 35 minutes rather than the 15 minutes he had guessed? Andrew now started to look sick which, from my point of view, was also a good sign. Continuing, I indicated to him that his record amounted to over 58 hours of lost time in the last year, and that 58 hours of lost time represented more time than his actual vacation represented in lost time to the company. This situation was creating a morale problem within his department, as well as causing the owner and Jackson considerable stress.

Andrew quickly replied yes when asked if he liked his job, stating that although there were some aspects of his work that he preferred over others, he really did like it for the most part. All this time, my violin case rested on the table. It was now time for it to play its part in this counseling session. I pointed to the case and asked Andrew if he had any idea what it was. He said that it looked like a violin case. I offered to show it to him if he liked and while he said okay, he had that "deer in the headlights" look. I opened the violin case, picked up the trashed fiddle, and handed it to him. As he looked at it closely, I asked him to tell me what he saw. He examined it and told me that it looked like a busted fiddle. I asked him to consider the fact that what he was holding was actually a 1794 Stradivarius violin, which in its present condition was worth a little over $5 million. His reaction was to cradle the violin in his hand a little bit more carefully. His pupils dilated and his eyes grew wide. I let him study the violin for about 25 or 30 seconds and told him that if the violin were restored, it would be worth around $50 million. His reaction was the same as most people's; he drew in his breath and held it. I let that soak in for another 30 seconds or so.

When asked, he willingly passed the violin back to me. I confessed that was not a Stradivarius violin, just a beat up fiddle worth almost nothing. It was a metaphor for his job. Some days your job may seem like a busted up fiddle, and there are lots of things you might think could be, and even should be, fixed to make the job better, easier, and more enjoyable. Correct? He agreed. I said, "But actually, even with all of its blemishes and detractions, it still a Stradivarius. Without the job, almost nothing else in your life would really work. The job provides the majority of funds to support your family, and provides you with your identity as a professional and as a wage earner. Correct?" He agreed again — his job was valuable and his assumption that he didn't have to be at work on time was putting it at risk.

I sat quietly for about a minute to let this point soak in. Making it clear to Andrew that his choice to retain an undependable car for his wife could have left him terminated, I told him that my objective was to help him understand the seriousness of the situation. My job was to structure terminations so that the company was protected against any recourse that the terminated employee might take to retaliate against the employer for wrongful termination. Good at my job, I would not allow his employer to exist in an indefensible position. Unemployment compensation for him would be about $195 to $245 a week. Could he live on that? Would he like to try? He said no.

Did he think he could rehabilitate his position with the company by coming to work each and every week on time starting the next day? He said yes. Agreeing with his decision, I said that I hoped he could because if he could not consistently arrive on time, I would be called back and the next time we saw each other, I would be terminating him. He looked at Jackson and assured him that the problem would be fixed. I thanked him and let him know that I would be documenting this as a written warning for his file. Telling him that the company did not expect perfection, I made it clear that it expected a lot more than he had delivered and suggested that for the next four months he set a goal of perfect attendance and punctuality. Perfection was a laudable goal, but the company could probably only tolerate one incident of tardiness per month. He understood, end of session.

Jackson said he appreciated my help and asked if he could borrow the fiddle when needed in the future which was fine with me. Next, I assisted him in completing the written documentation of the written warning. The first paragraph needed to stipulate "what went wrong." The second paragraph needed to specify what the company policy or expectations were, as well as perhaps the company's values. The final paragraph needed to clearly state the plan of corrective action and its timetable including consequences that could be expected to follow should it not be achieved. We drafted the following:

MEMO

To: Personnel File

Fr: Steve Cohen, HR Consultant & xxxx, COO

Date: xxxx

Re: Andrew, tardiness, written warning

On XXX date, we met with Andrew. The purpose of the meeting was to inform Andrew that we had completed a time card audit and had documented the existence of a significant problem. A copy of the time card audit is attached to this memo. We advised Andrew that his attendance contained a consistent problem, specifically that he arrived late to work. The time card audit demonstrated that Andrew was late approximately 100 times during the past year. Additionally, each instance of tardiness contained an average of 35 minutes. This experience amounted to approximately 3500 minutes or 58+ hours of lost time due to tardiness.

We advised Andrew that the company could not function efficiently or effectively with this kind of employee behavior. We advised that we recognized that legitimate circumstances exist causing employees to be late for work from time to time. There is a tolerance for an occasional tardiness or even an occasional absence. The company expects its employees to demonstrate an attitude that shows they are engaged and that they prioritize the company's needs for high productivity. Andrew was provided a copy of the company policy specifying its expectations that all employees arrive on their schedule at their appointed time with regularity and consistency.

We advised Andrew that, beginning immediately, and extending for the next 120 days, he would be expected to arrive every day on schedule and on time. If he is going to be late for any reason, he has to notify his supervisor, and provide notice and an explanation. Andrew was advised that no more than one incident of tardiness per month would be tolerated. We hoped that all incidences of tardiness during the probationary period could be eliminated. We further advised Andrew that if he was unable to meet these expectations that further disciplinary action, up to and including termination, could result.

Andrew said that he understood our expectations and would endeavor to rehabilitate his reputation and status with the company.

At the close of the case, I marked my calendar and four months later called Jackson to inquire into the status of Andrew's probation. I was advised that Andrew bought himself a new car and gave his old, but still dependable, car to his wife. This evidently solved the problem, and Andrew had been at work and on time consistently through the probationary period. Jackson asked me if he should remove the write-up from Andrew's personnel file since he had completed his probationary period satisfactorily. I told him absolutely not, that the document was to be a permanent record and reminded him that if there were a relapse or backsliding, he would need to document it. I suggested that Curt draft a statement for Andrew's file indicating that he had successfully completed his probationary period, that the company expected Andrew to continue to show up on time, and that they would also continue to monitor his attendance on a regular basis. The bottom line was that while Andrew's formal probation ended, the expectation for his ongoing performance was still present.

The case concluded with Andrew getting the message that the company cared about him and the details associated with his job. I ended up developing a comprehensive personnel policies and procedure manual, which was, installed company wide. There was a time around the late 1980s that companies were encouraged not to have formal personnel policies because then they were being held accountable in the courts and by the DOL if they failed to follow their own policies. As a result, some companies adopted a posture that they would just do away with policies so, therefore, they couldn't be held accountable to follow them. The end result was that practices could be applied or changed on an arbitrary and capricious basis. The courts and the EEOC soon figured this out and adopted the premise that employees could not formally be held accountable for practices, only for policies.

Management Messages

1. Due process, once again, is a significant issue with multiple aspects to know and consider. To start, know that it includes an oral warning, a written warning, and then suspension or termination. These are the required steps as specified by the DOL. The courts and the DOL require or expect employers to provide due process as a vehicle for achieving corrective action. Employers, when they discover or determine that an employee is not performing, are expected to tell the employee that he or she is not performing adequately, tell the employee what it is that needs to be done differently or better, and then give time to make the change or improvement. If improvement is not noted, the employer is again expected to tell the employee what is wrong, how to fix it, and again give time to show improvement. If after these two steps improvement is still not demonstrated, then the employer may terminate the employee. The first time around is an oral warning, which is not considered disciplinary action. The second time is a written warning, and it is technically the first step in disciplinary or corrective action.

    When documenting the various steps associated with due process or corrective action, I recommend a specific format. I recommend that the document actually be addressed to the personnel file rather than the individual employee. The heading of the document looks like this:

> Line 1: MEMO
> Line 2: To: Personnel File
> Line 3: Fr: supervisor's name
> Line 4: date document was written
> Line 5: Re: written warning for specify employee's name

The reason I recommend addressing the documentation to "personnel file" is that it is more professional and less personal than addressing the memo to the individual employee. Another point is that the personnel file is clearly owned by the company and as its property, the company has more control over it. If the document were written to the employee, then technically the employee should have or could have greater control over the document, who sees it, and how it's used. Another suggestion for the document is that it is written in third party format. For example, the document should not read: I spoke with you about coming in late. He said he understood the severity of the issue. The document should rather be written as: I spoke with Mr. Jones about coming in late. He said he understood the severity of his situation.

Once the document has been written and shared with the employee, it should be placed in the employee's permanent record. Permanent record means *permanent* record. Once it's placed in the file, it should not be removed or discarded. Usually the document will specify a time period. An example might be that the employee is placed on probation for the next six months. The employee is given this period of time to demonstrate consistently good performance or behavior. If he or she fails to demonstrate consistently good performance or behavior, the document should specify, "Further disciplinary action up to and including termination could result." Let's say that the employee successfully completes the probationary period. The document should not be withdrawn, but rather a new document should be drafted. The new document should say that the employee has successfully completed his or her probationary period. It should further say that the employee's performance will continue to be monitored and is expected to remain consistently successful or productive. If the original document were to be removed at the successful conclusion of the probationary period, then management has created a situation that it doesn't want. The paper trail would be lost as there would be no proof of the written warning. The record should show the chronology: there was a problem, the problem was identified to the employee, and the employee was able to fix the problem. No documents should ever be removed from the employee's personnel file.

2. The difference between a practice and a policy also warrants expansion. The lowest or most elementary form of organizational behavior is a practice. The next level of organizational behavior up would be a policy. An example might be: It is our practice to check email on an intermittent basis. A policy might be: Email in our organization is not private and should be restricted to business communication. We reserve the right to monitor email if we consider it appropriate to do so.

   This difference between a practice and a policy is significant. It is similar to the difference between inadvertent and overt behavior. A policy is a practice that has been thought through and then formalized. The DOL and the courts have asserted that employees cannot be held legally accountable to practices — only policies. I recommend to my clients that they have formally stated personnel policies and that these policies are formally communicated to their employees. Once policies have been established and communicated, then they can be imposed. Once imposed, employees can be held accountable to follow the policies. Additionally, management has to follow the policies they set up. If the policies are not consistently applied, an issue of favoritism or discrimination can be created.

Chapter 9

Health Issues and the Law: Two Cases — Two Pariahs

Addressing performance problems with employees who have health-related issues is a very serious matter. The courts and the DOL consistently come down, really hard, on employers who mess with employees who are ill.

The Americans with Disabilities Act (ADA), the Pregnancy Leave Act (PLA), and the Family Medical Leave Act (FMLA), just to mention a few, all exist to protect employees from their employers. That said, not all organizations are held accountable to provide their employees with these protections. For example, the employee group must exceed 15 in order for the employer to be required to provide ADA benefits, and there must be at least 49 employees for the benefits of FMLA to kick in. Most employees know their rights under these laws.

The ADA requires the employer to grant the employee up to 12 weeks of absence due to an illness (the employee's or a member of the employee's family) as long as the ill person is under the care of a licensed medical practitioner. The illness could be physical, like the result of an accident or injury, or it could be mental, such as stress. There is no distinction between the two in the law. During this absence, the employee can burn through all their paid sick and vacation leave. If they have exhausted their paid leave but still require time away, and they are under the 12-week (per year) maximum, the balance of the leave can be unpaid. The important thing is that the employer must hold the job open and available to the employee when he or she returns. There are some very narrow exceptions, but for most employees this amounts to job protection for up to a 12-week period. And, this benefit reestablishes itself every 12 months!

Remember that there are three kinds of behaviors. There is overt behavior which is planned, inadvertent or autopilot behavior, and opportunistic or predatory behavior. A good example of opportunistic behavior in a health-related situation is when an employee goes to his or her doctor and advises that he or she is super stressed because of all the pressure at work. The obvious answer is that the employee needs to get away from work to reduce this stress. The doctor writes the order, and the employee goes back to the employer with the doctor's order for time off. The employer is obligated to grant the medical leave.

So, the employee goes home and puts his or her feet up. Say that this employee has accumulated 160 hours of sick leave benefits over time. This translates into the first four weeks of the stress-related medical leave as paid time off. By "coincidence," just as the 160 hours of paid time has been exhausted, the employee feels well enough to return to work. Shortly after he or she returns to work, a voluntary resignation is submitted as the employee has accepted another position. Under the law and the policies of this person's employer, he or she knows that pay will be received for all accumulated vacation benefits, but that sick leave benefits go unpaid at termination. So, under the protection of the ADA, the employee has accessed all the sick time benefits prior to his or her voluntary resignation. That's predatory and opportunistic behavior, wouldn't you say? And unfortunately, there is nothing that the employer can do.

There are lots of variations on this little plan. Take the alcoholic or drug addict. So long as the drunk or the junkie is under the care of his or her physician, the employer is obliged to accommodate the requirements for time off from work and the employee is protected from termination. Combine this with the requirement of the law to provide the employee with strict confidentiality, and you have the employer with both hands tied with regard to holding this employee accountable.

Because most business owners, especially small business owners, are so singularly focused on productivity, they are appalled to learn of all the limitations placed upon them by government rules and regulations. Let me provide a couple of examples. There was a small community bank that employed about 50 people. One of the tellers was an African- American woman, Helen, who was about 34 years old. She was a three pack a day smoker who had developed a hacking smoker's cough. Several times a day, she would launch into a coughing fit that could last as long as 60 or 90 seconds. At first blush, that might not seem like a long time, but when witnessed, it can appear like a medical emergency lasting an eternity. Imagine if this woman beside you, as a coworker, launched into a 90 second coughing fit in which she turned red and couldn't get her breath. At first, it was a disconcerting and disquieting experience in which more than one coworker felt obligated to call 911. After so many of these experiences, coworkers transitioned from being concerned to being annoyed and then to becoming hostile.

Now, imagine customers in the bank standing in front of this teller when she launches into her coughing fit. This is a new, first-time experience for the customer whose natural initial response is concern. After all, Helen looks like she's choking, which of course she is! The customer becomes seriously concerned and wants something done and looks around to the other bank employees for help. Meanwhile, the coworkers are exhibiting either disregard or contempt for this employee who is in obvious distress. Real bad PR, wouldn't you say?

Management had a real problem. Helen had the right to smoke so long as it was confined to the appropriate place and time. She could not help the fact that she launched into these coughing fits. It was not her choice or something she enjoyed, just part of the burden of being a heavy smoker. While Helen was under the care of a physician who had urged her to quit smoking, she hadn't, couldn't, or wouldn't. What was management to do? They called me.

The exasperated owner, Ben, and branch manager, Alan, briefed me on the situation. On the one hand, the teller was a competent employee, but on the other hand, she was creating havoc. Her peers had turned against her and were no longer sympathetic. The customers, when confronted with the coughing, were very concerned and negative PR was resulting. At work, Helen was becoming a pariah. As customary, after my scope documents were written and approved, I endeavored to interview those making the allegations — the other tellers. What I found was that even the most charitable of the coworkers was aggravated. Interview after interview, coworker after coworker, all were frustrated. Most were completely grossed out by the hacking and spitting of sputum, and others were annoyed by the many smoke breaks and the smell of tobacco and nicotine that permeated her clothes and persona. All wanted the situation to improve, and none had a solution short of getting rid of her. I learned that these episodes could occur as often as two or three times during a regular eight-hour shift. They could be brief, lasting only five or 10 seconds, or they could go on for up to 90. It was a huge disruption, and almost no one was sympathetic by this point. During one of my coworker interviews, I did have the opportunity to observe one of the coughing fits. It was not pretty.

I then interviewed Helen. During the 40-minute interview, I could smell the smoke on her clothes and breath. Thankfully, she did not go into a hacking fit during my confined time with her. Helen told me that she had tried to quit and had actually cut down to a little over two packs a day. She knew it was bad for her and that it was harming her career, but she just did not know what to do. Very much aware of the problem, she realized that most of her coworkers were mad at her, and the ones that were once friends had become distant. Being at work wasn't the most pleasant part of her day, but she needed the money to go to school and pay her bills. A strong and resolute woman, she seemed reconciled that she wouldn't have any friends at work and was actually migrating toward her own sense of animosity toward her coworkers. They, she concluded, were obviously insensitive toward her so she was constructing firewalls as a coping mechanism. She knew her rights under the law and was determined to show up every day and do her job regardless of her coughing and its influence on others.

Asking Helen about her future plans and her area of study at school, she told me she was getting her degree in accounting and anticipated becoming an auditor. She had three semesters to go, but working necessitated going to school on a part-time basis so her degree would probably take two or more years to complete. I immediately recognized this career as a good choice for her because she would have limited interaction with her coworkers. As an auditor, she would be out in the field working with client accounts and have limited contact with them, as she would be sequestered in private areas reviewing financial records and inventories. This seemed pretty doable considering her smoking burden.

Like a BB in a boxcar, I now had the makings of a remedy rattling around in my brain. I met with Alan and Ben and informed them that Helen had certainly polarized her workmates against her. I had not spoken with any of the bank's customers but could certainly understand their reaction to witnessing one of these spells. I told them that I did not see the situation getting any better as the hacking and coughing spells were not seasonal and could be expected to continue and get worse. Helen was not breaking any laws, and in fact, was protected by several laws. When I confirmed that the coworkers were disenchanted with this situation to say the very least, the president asked me to tell them something they didn't know. I was not surprised that my conclusions were not revelations to this astute man or his branch manager.

I informed them that if they terminated her, she had the personality and presence to exercise her rights to recourse. She could certainly assert a wrongful discharge or wrongful termination case and could probably prevail in the courts or with the EEOC. There would be very little sympathy for the bank in a case like this. Ben interjected that he had to do something as customers were put off enough to leave the bank, and employees were aggravated enough to complain at the very least and, more likely, to leave in protest. Not only were they repulsed by the coughing fits, customers were looking to them to do something. This was awkward to say the least since there was nothing they could do and no way to let the customers know. I agreed that something needed to be done, and I had a solution. They were all ears.

Being a teller at this bank was only a means to the ends as Helen was aspiring to become an accountant I said, filling the owner and branch manager in on her goal, an important part of my plan. Defending against a wrongful discharge lawsuit could cost the bank between $50,000 and $150,000, and Helen was in two protected classes in that she was a minority female, and she had a health-related problem. She was smart and articulate and would be a credible adversary. I suggested that we needed to avoid a battle and seek her voluntary resignation as well as her signature on a hold harmless waiver in return for assisting her with her school and living expenses. The president was open to my suggestion and told me to get back to him as quickly as possible with the approximate cost, information that turned out to be fairly easy to obtain. Books and tuition at her school would be about $3,000 per semester. In addition to the $9000 in direct costs, a stipend of $250 per month for the year, $3000, could be offered. We should make that offer to Helen in exchange for her cooperation in exiting her employment at the bank.

I told them that the courts and the government considered healthcare matters as sacrosanct. They take a very dim view of owners and operators taking action against employees due to the employee's health-related problems. Not only would Helen prevail in this situation, but the bad PR in the marketplace that could result would obviously have a deleterious impact on the bank's business. Telling Ben that his values were on display with this and every other decision that he made, I encouraged him to assist this employee in her endeavors to move on. The $12,000 expense in extricating her, along with my fee, would be a small price to pay to solve this problem. He reluctantly agreed and approved my plan to negotiate with Helen. We agreed that the branch manager and I would meet with her the next day at the beginning of her shift. Then, I would suspend her with pay in order to create the environment and time necessary to introduce my plan.

When Alan and I met with Helen the next morning, I explained that the situation had reached a point where the bank had no choice but to terminate the employment relationship. I told her that she was correct in her assumptions about her standing with her coworkers and asked her if she was aware of the impact she was having on them as well as customers. She responded that she did. Proceeding, I anonymously provided details of the results of my interviews with her coworkers and also told her about the bank's concerns relative to customer comments. The bank had no choice but to sever their relationship.

Now was the time to suggest an alternative. The bank had no interest in harming her or stifling her future endeavors. In fact, the bank had an idea to help her. With her interest perked, she invited me to proceed. I told her that I had been thinking about what she was planning for her career and that it was a good field for her. In addition, I told her that I hoped her health improved, but even if it didn't, her career plans seemed like they could be accommodated even under these circumstances. Just because she couldn't continue at the bank didn't mean that the bank didn't want her to continue with her career plans, which would, of course, necessitate her finishing school. Now I really had her attention, and I wasted no time letting her know that the bank would like to offer her scholarship, books, and tuition for her three remaining semesters.

She was thrilled with the prospect. I told her that the bank would provide her with $3000 per semester for three semesters if she would voluntary resign and sign a hold harmless waiver. I decided not to offer the additional $3000 knowing that I could add it to the pot should it become necessary to close the deal. Helen was told that she could think about it, and I suggested we could get together the next day to discuss further details. For now, she could leave her personal items and take the rest of the day off with pay to consider the bank's offer. She agreed to meet me the following day.

I provided a brief report to Ben and assured him that we were on track with more information to come after tomorrow's meeting. I did not tell him about holding back the $3000. The next day Helen met me as scheduled. Chipper and upbeat, she told me that she felt grateful that the bank was willing to take such a generous position considering the turbulence she had caused. She went so far as to say the offer seemed too good to be true and asked to look at the hold harmless agreement. It had been drafted to be fairly simple and straightforward, and she saw that it contained no onerous clauses or requirements. It basically stated that she agreed not to take any adverse action against the bank, and the bank agreed not to take any adverse action against her. In addition, Helen agreed not to say anything against the bank, and the bank agreed not to say anything against her. She accepted the offer, signed the document, and asked if she could thank the bank's owner personally. I said yes and told her I would have the first increment of $3,000 available within a week. Her final paycheck, plus her accrued vacation hours, would be coming out on the next regular payday, and her personal items would be available to her when I delivered the first check.

I proceeded back to the bank and presented Ben and Alan with the signed agreement pointing out that I got the deal closed at an actual savings over the approved amount and took the opportunity to pass on Helen's statement that she would be calling with a personal thank you. I suggested that the branch manager speak with the staff and inform them that Helen voluntarily resigned. Obviously, none of the details surrounding her departure could be divulged, but he could say that she left happy because the bank took the high road. There was no termination so there could be no wrongful termination action taken against the bank. All's well that ends well!

The next case involved an individual that most people, including myself, found to be personally objectionable. It wasn't his looks; it was his persona. His looks were particularly unattractive, but I always try to look past that find something about the person that is likable or laudable. It is, in fact, important for me to find that aspect and concentrate on it in the process of closing a case. I am working to build a bridge and acting as an advocate, creating a bond to make negotiations smooth and beneficial to all parties.

If you have children, think back to when they were young and the times they brought their friends over to the house. Remember those instances? You may recall that there were some that you just found to be objectionable. For some reason, you just did not like them. There were other friends invited over who you really enjoyed. They could do no wrong, and you might have even found yourself visiting or snacking between meals with them just to be in their company. This is just human nature. Some people are attractive to us, and others just repel us. The individual in this case, Mason, had that immediate negative affect on me. He was extremely tall, perhaps 6' 6" and gave the impression of the character in the James Bond movie entitled *Moon Raker* named Jaws. He didn't have those braces that looked like they were on steroids, but he did have that kind of longish hair and the same ghoulish and macabre smile.

Mason had a very appropriate job for person with his personality. He was a parking lot security person on the campus of a major university. Driving around all day monitoring the cars in the eighty or so parking lots, he gave out tickets to those who didn't have the appropriate permit for that particular lot. This was a fitting job for him as Mason did have an affliction that affected his social interaction. He had a disease that isn't particularly well understood but is legitimate non-the-less. It's called Tourette's Syndrome and can manifest itself in quirky, herky-jerky, involuntary movements of various parts of the body. It can also manifest itself orally causing the individual to utter words or sounds involuntarily. Sometimes the utterances come out as profanity. Again, it's a disease that is relatively rare in the workplace, Because it can manifest itself as inadvertent antisocial outbursts, it can cause the victim to be socially isolated and interpersonally immature. Mason's Tourette's manifested itself in a particularly gross and antisocial way. He found himself picking his nose involuntarily. So nice. This behavior, because it is an involuntary manifestation of Tourette's, is protected behavior under the ADA. What that means is that he can pick his nose all day long in front of anybody or everybody, and it cannot be held against him from an employment perspective. Mason, in my opinion, used his disability as a shield to justify this and other behaviors and choices that were perfectly voluntary.

The university's vice chancellor for administration hired me. He supervised the director of campus security, Edgar, who had advised him that there was a problem within his department. Subsequently, Edgar was directed by his boss to use me. He told me that he intended to fire Mason and that he really did not need my help. Heavy emphasis on the word "help." I asked him why he was talking to me then, and he said flatly, "Orders." I'm glad

I had friends in high places at this university, and I informed Edgar that since he was stuck with me, he at least ought to let me earn my keep. He humored me by providing me with the background on Mason.

He said that Mason was a complete asshole who creeped out everyone with whom he came in contact. This included students, visitors, and faculty to whom he gave parking tickets, along with his coworkers and supervisors. "At least he's being consistent," I commented. Seeing no humor in the situation, Edgar continued by providing examples of complaints from each of the three sources. He told me that, in his opinion, he had enough to terminate Mason and warned me that I could do whatever I wanted to do as long as I didn't get in the way of his plans to terminate. I thanked Edgar and told him that I would keep him informed. Would he advise those in the office that I would be speaking with them and of my authorization to do so? He didn't answer, but I knew he would comply — he had been told to cooperate.

My first stop was Mason's immediate supervisor, Paul. I expected this guy to be a junior Edgar Hoover. He really wasn't. Paul was pretty down to earth, kind of a "live and let live" kind of person. He told me that he had been in this job for three years and had just completed his bachelor's degree in criminal justice. He had hired Mason 13 months ago. When asked if Mason did a competent job, he said, "Yes, to a degree." He was dependable and knew the department's policies and procedures, but he also had some problems. "For instance," I said, encouraging him to continue. For example, he was assigned a golf cart to use to get around campus as he had a large number of parking lots to monitor and control. Due to inattentiveness, he had had two accidents with his golf cart. The first accident banged up the cart. In the second accident, he almost hit a pedestrian as well as banged up the cart. After the second accident, the cart was taken away, and Mason was expected to patrol his assigned parking lots on foot. Paul conceded that he should have used the second incident to terminate Mason, but he did not. He suggested it was misplaced mercy.

Paul went on to say that he had received numerous complaints from faculty, students, staff, and visitors about Mason, three of which were in writing. The complaints were mostly about Mason appearing to enjoy giving tickets to parking offenders. They also revolved around his creepy personal appearance and his public display of nose picking. Paul rightly assessed these complaints as accurate, and he correctly understood his limitations relative to dealing with these complaints. He tried to provide Mason with customer service training and counseling to get him to dial down his obvious pleasure associated with giving out parking tickets. Mason insisted that the nose picking was part of his Tourette's, which he couldn't help. He also asserted that he couldn't help what he looked like, and that if he appeared creepy to others, it wasn't his problem. He wore a clean uniform, combed his hair, and bathed regularly. The supervisor was exasperated with him but was also smart enough to realize that this was a pretty complicated situation. I thanked him for his time and acknowledged that he was correct in his presumption that the situation was indeed complicated and required extreme care.

My next interview was with the department's dispatcher. She was a young and attractive coed, Chloe, working in the security department to earn money while working her way through school. I told her that this was a confidential personnel matter and asked her to describe her feelings and any experiences she had had with Mason. Chloe was unabashed and forthright. She told me that she didn't like him and was, again, creeped out by almost everything about him. His constant, nasty personal habit and his disregard for her feelings or wishes grossed her out. I told her that I understood the nose picking part, but asked her to elaborate the part about disregarding her feelings and wishes. She said that she hated rap music, which Mason happened to love. He would come into the office, wink at her, actually more like a leer then a wink, and then break into a rap song. She called it his "rectal recital." So cute. Chloe told me that, on many occasions, she asked him not to rap around her because she didn't like it and hated the words, but he continued to do it just to annoy her. At the time, I did not pursue the comment about Mason leering at her, but it was lodged securely in my brain.

There were three other parking lot monitors who occupied the same title and position as Mason. I talked to each one of them individually, and individually they confirmed that Mason was the department's outcast as he annoyed them and everyone else with whom he came in contact. He openly talked about his Tourette's when he first joined the department, so they were well aware of his condition and thought he got way too much leniency from the supervisor because of it. However, they liked their boss, and they even liked Edgar. From a staff of over 15 campus security officers, I spoke with two or three as sort of a spot check. They knew Mason and saw him as a misfit, but a harmless one. I was told that most people started in the department in the parking lot patrol and used that as a springboard into the security officer classification. They said that Mason seemed to like his job even though it was a dead end in his situation; it was as good as it was going to get for that guy. They too were aware of his Tourette's because he talked about it openly to everybody who would listen.

Now that I had satisfied my usual procedure of interviewing the person or persons making the complaints, I made an appointment to interview Mason. I told him that I was there to complete an inquiry into the concerns that his supervisor and coworkers had regarding his suitability for his position. He immediately launched into an explanation that he could not help what others felt about him. He told me about his Tourette's and how he would discover that his finger was up his nose without his being aware of it until after the fact. He said that he couldn't stop it, and it was just a fact of his life he and others would have to deal with. I could tell that Mason had some experience with the kind of confrontation that I was mounting. He told me that he was under a doctor's care, and he knew his rights under the ADA. Mason said that his supervisor understood his Tourette's and had made an accommodation.

Perhaps some background is appropriate at this point. The Americans with Disabilities Act (ADA), requires employers, once they are advised that their employee has a physical or mental condition, to consider making a "reasonable accommodation" so that the employee can continue in his or her job. The ADA does not require the employer to make the accommodation, only to consider making it. If the employer determines that the requested accommodation is reasonable, and makes a reasonable accommodation which corrects the problem, then hopefully the matter is under control. An example might be an employee who has limited vision and asks his or her employer to furnish a special phone with an enlarged keypad. This would be deemed a reasonable accommodation. If the same employee requested the company hire a person to dial the phone for him or her, this request would probably be denied as unreasonable. If the employer considers the requested accommodation to be unreasonable and denies it, the impaired employee has an avenues of recourse available. He or she can file a complaint with the DOL claiming there is a dispute and an investigation is then precipitated. As has been stated on numerous occasions, the courts, the states, and the federal government take a very dim view of the employers taking adverse action against employees due to their health conditions. These ADA challenges are costly and usually result in bad PR for the employer. The employer might as well stand in quicksand.

Getting back to Mason, he had let me know that his aunt was a lawyer with a daughter who had recently been diagnosed with Tourette's. He told me that his aunt would probably like to have a conversation with me to help me understand the law as it applied to him and asked for my card, which I had no problem providing. Clearly a thinly veiled threat.

Sensing it was a good time to change direction, I asked Mason if he liked rap music, to which he responded that it was his favorite thing in the entire world. He loved it and was fascinated by rap artists. In answer to a question about his favorite artists and songs, he rattled off a few names, none of which rang any bells with me. I asked him to "sing" his favorite rap song for me. Mason proceeded to launch into this "song." It wasn't really a song, more like a vile poem that denigrated women, referring to them as whores to be used in a variety of disgusting sexual ways. I asked him if this song was the one he sang when he was in the department office, and he confirmed that he sang that song, and others like it, on a regular basis. Was he sure that he sang that song at the office? He said yes. I asked him if he remembered singing that song, or others like it, in Chloe's presence. He said "Probably, yes." He also answered yes when asked if was aware she didn't like it and admitted she had told him so. Finally, I asked him why he continued to sing his rap music in her presence knowing that she didn't like it, and he said that he really liked to "push her buttons." Interesting. I told him that I would get back to him in the near future.

I then went back to Mason's supervisor and asked him to call Chloe into his office for a meeting with us. When she arrived, I asked her to recall, if she could, any of the words that were contained in any of the rap songs that Mason sang while in her presence. She told me that they were the typical crap (her words) of most rap music: violence, sex, and anger toward women and white people. When asked if she felt offended by the words of the songs, Chloe said that she tried to ignore what he was saying and doing when he was in the office. She didn't pay close attention, just tried to focus on her work, and he would eventually move on. Chloe indicated that she didn't, and wouldn't, allow him to torture her.

Continuing to talk to Paul, I told him that I saw a way to extricate Mason without it spilling over to his Tourette's. I had his attention. Upon perusing Mason's personnel file, I found two very competent and thorough write-ups regarding the two accidents with the golf cart. There were three copies of letters, two from staff personnel, and one from a student, complaining about his lack of customer service skills. The documentation trail was pretty good. I suggested that we go to see Edgar.

In the meeting with Edgar, I advised him that I had completed my investigation and substantiated the allegations that Mason was an asshole. I said that, unfortunately, being an asshole is not a termination offense. I could see that Edgar was starting to get that irritated look on his face when informed that Mason not only clearly understood his rights under the ADA but also had an aunt who was a lawyer whose daughter was just recently diagnosed with her own case of Tourette's. She was probably going to call me but not to worry; there would be no intimidation.

Paul asked whether the information about the aunt's daughter was significant. I suggested that she would be like any other parent when confronted with the fact that a child had a disease. She would be freaked out. Since she is familiar with Tourette's because of Mason and aware of the reaction of others towards him, she would have an understanding of what her daughter would face. I guessed that this aunt would intercede in Mason's case with tremendous force as preparation for what she would need to protect her own daughter. Paul had a resigned look on his face. Even Edgar looked a bit discouraged.

While I did have an idea, it would require us to be a bit creative. I said that there was no way that the inappropriate social behavior could be used as a vehicle for termination. While his "nose habit" was gross and antisocial, it was still protected under the ADA because it was directly attributable to his disability. His enthusiasm for giving tickets was also not actionable because that was his job. Finally, even his generally creepy appearance and demeanor were not actionable. Certainly, his lack of customer service skills could be actionable, but that would take a lot of time and involve a lot of people registering complaints against him.

I told them about Mason's launching into rap music over the objections of the dispatcher. While she certainly was not the only one who had problems with Mason, she was the one who offered a solution to the dilemma of how to get Mason out without opening the door to a wrongful discharge lawsuit due to the Tourette's. I offered the definition of sexual harassment by hostile work environment. Sexual harassment was unwelcome, unsolicited, and unreciprocated behavior of a sexual nature. For the charge of hostile work environment to be invoked, there must be a pattern of offensive, unwelcome behavior of a sexual nature. Since the words to the rap songs were denigrating toward women and had sexuality at their core, the rap music that Mason selected and directed toward Chloe could be easily construed as behavior of a sexual nature. Since she had asked Mason to discontinue his "music" concerts, and he had disregarded her requests to cease and desist, I felt that he had reached and crossed the threshold of sexual harassment. This, coupled with the various complaints documented in his file and the two accidents with the golf cart clearly indicated that Mason's employment was unsustainable.

What we needed was for Chloe to understand her role if the termination of Mason were contested. She might need to stand up and provide deposition and oral testimony that she was far more than just annoyed by his behavior as she had indicated during our interview. For this to reach the level of sexual harassment by hostile work environment, she would have to be offended. I told them that, if I were successful in doing my work, no termination would result. If there were no termination, there could be no wrongful termination and therefore no follow up recourse could occur. However, I told them that there was always the slight possibility that a formal fight could result, given the lawyer aunt's possible intercession. We would just have to see. They told me that they would talk with Chloe and let me know in the near future.

The very next day, I got the expected call from the aunt. She was very professional and quite condescending advising me of what the ADA required of the employer and the various protections it provided for her nephew. She told me that she was licensed to practice law in this particular state and that she would not hesitate to file a lawsuit if he was terminated. I assured her that the employer was well aware of its responsibilities under the law and that the employer would take no action against her nephew due to his behavior as it related to his Tourette's. That was against the law, against the employer's policies, and against the employer's values to take any action against an employee because of his or her health condition, Mason had advised me that her daughter had been recently diagnosed with Tourette's and that, as a parent, she had my sympathy. She thanked me, and again reminded me to caution the university to be very careful how they handled her nephew. Thanking her, I bid her good day.

Another day passed and Edgar called requesting my presence for a meeting. Chloe had reconsidered her position and was prepared, if necessary, to file a formal complaint of sexual harassment against Mason. I recommended that we meet with Mason. My plan was to advise him that we intended to terminate him. Edgar agreed but he was not willing to provide any severance package. I prevailed upon him to follow the university's overly generous policy, which was to provide 30 days pay for every year of service if there was sufficient cause to offer a severance package. I encouraged him to reconsider, as it would be smart to allow Mason to vacate voluntarily if he would, with the severance package as a sweetener if required.

Later that day, Paul and I made an appointment to speak with Mason. He lumbered into the office and plopped himself into the chair next to me and across from his supervisor. He was picking his nose and had that silly "I'm bulletproof" look on his face as he asked what we had in mind. I had arranged with Paul to let me to do all the talking and started by relaying the conversation with his aunt from the other day. That seemed to please him and he asked, "Then what we got talk about?" I told him that the security department had decided to terminate the employment relationship between them; his record over the previous year had not been sterling. Normally, in this situation, I do not rehash the employee's "wall of shame," but in this case, I thought it was quite appropriate. Not wanting him to entertain the wrong idea, I made it clear that the reasons for his termination had nothing to do with his disability or its symptoms. The causes of his termination had to be understood. We walked through the two accidents with the golf cart and the three letters of complaint from his fan base. Then I told him that the most serious of the strikes against him was the substantiated allegation of sexual harassment by hostile work environment. His back stiffened, his finger came out of his nose, and the smug, but casual, look on his face was replaced with the classic look of "Oh my God!"

Mason was informed that the university had a zero tolerance policy regarding sexual harassment. Explaining the definition of sexual harassment and specifically the definition of sexual harassment by hostile work environment to him, I said that singing the songs that contained words he had admitted he used was offensive to the dispatcher. I reminded him that Chloe had asked him, on several occasions, to refrain from singing songs with the offensive language. On each of those occasions, he chose to disregard her requests and continue his behavior. While he might think he was merely annoying her, he was actually sexually harassing her. I assured Mason that since he had admitted to doing this, the university had an ironclad case against him. Pausing, I let that sink in for a minute.

The next time I spoke, I said that the university was a benevolent employer and had no interest in harming him or his career in any way. The university was willing to offer him an alternative to being terminated. The standard release waiver I had prepared was then slid across the table. I told him that he should fax the document to his aunt, and she could explain it to him and provide counsel. It basically said that if he voluntarily resigned and signed the "hold harmless" waiver, the university would accept his resignation, promise not to reveal his poor work record and this incident, and provide him with two weeks pay. If he wanted to, he could have his aunt call me directly. She already had my number.

He stood up, put his finger in his nose, took the document, and walked out of the office. He must've been from Florida because he uttered something to me about the "sun on the beach" Somehow, I don't think it was complimentary. I told the supervisor that I would handle things from here who then told me he felt better already.

Later that day, I got the expected call from the aunt. Still very professional and still rather condescending in her tone of voice, she asked me if I thought the employer could win the legal battle that was brewing. I assured her that we were very sure that we could win the battle if he chose to wage it, since he had admitted to singing the rap songs. This admission, along with the presence of an eyewitness, pretty much made the case. Asking her if she was familiar with her nephew' choice of music, I inquired whether she would like me to download and send her a few samples of his favorite songs. I assured her that playing these songs that he was so fond of, in the open court would have a huge impact on the outcome of the case. We spent about 45 minutes on the phone, most of it consisting of me attempting to convince her that it was not in her nephew's best interests to take his employer into court. I reminded her that Mason was a young man with a disability. Having a record that included filing a lawsuit against his employer, coupled with the public disclosure of his less than sterling employee record via a reference check, could cripple his chances of obtaining future employment. By voluntarily resigning and signing the hold harmless waiver, the university was willing to assist her nephew with an expunged record, a neutral reference, and a small severance package.

In the end, she asked me to double the severance package to four weeks pay and include an additional month's health insurance coverage. Since

I already had approval to provide up to four weeks pay in the severance support package, I told her that if she waved the sunset provision in the agreement, we had a deal. All these agreements contain what is called a sunset provision. It means once the document is presented, the signer has up to 21 days to consider the offer and then an additional seven days after signing the document to rescind the agreement. This period is called the sunset clause. She agreed that he would sign the document immediately and wave the seven-day sunset. I told her that I would get back with her after I discussed it with the employer.

I called Edgar and Paul and told them that we had reached an agreement. Mason would sign the letter of resignation and the hold harmless waiver within the next few days. The deal was done, the resignation would stick, and there would be no wrongful termination lawsuit. I have to admit that I presumed that Edgar would, at least, say thank you. In fact, what happened was there was a long pause after I delivered the good news, and when Edgar finally spoke, he said he had to take another call holding on the other line. He hung up and Paul apologized for Edger's rudeness and offered congratulations. I accepted his thanks and asked him to pull Mason's personal items together so that I could deliver them when I collected the signed documents. He assured me that they would be ready in 24 hours.

I called the vice chancellor who had hired me in the first place and told him that the deal was done and permanently closed. There would be no legal action taken against the university. He said he would love to hear the whole story, perhaps over lunch someday, thanked me and told me to submit my invoice.

Management Lessons

1. I have said many times throughout this book that the courts and the DOL take a very dim view of employers who take steps against employees due to health- related matters. There are many laws or rules that provide rights and protections in this area. There is the ADA (the Americans with Disabilities Act) and the FMLA

(Family Medical Leave Act). An employer must employ 15 or more employees to be accountable to the ADA. The employer must employ 50 or more employees to be accountable to FMLA. There are some additional caveats including the length of time the employee has been employed to be eligible for the specific law. The ADA requires the employer to *consider* providing a "reasonable accommodation" to an employee who has a mental or physical disability. The employer is not required to provide the accommodation but is required to consider a request for an accommodation. It must be documented by the employer that the employer has received a request for an accommodation. Then it must be documented that the employer considered it and made the decision to grant the accommodation because it was reasonable or to deny the accommodation because it was considered unreasonable.

2. FMLA requires the employer to grant the employee a paid or unpaid medical leave of absence if there is a bona fide need for that medical leave of absence. FMLA requires the employer to protect the employee's job — in other words hold the job open and available to the employee when he or she returns from the medical leave providing the medical leave was 12 weeks or less. If the medical leave extends beyond 12 weeks, the employer is not required to reinstate the employee.

3. One of the most important elements of FMLA is that it needs to be formally invoked. When the employer determines that a medical leave is going to be necessary, in other words the employee is going to need to be gone for some extended period of time, then the employee's FMLA rights need to be invoked in writing. This could be as simple as a registered letter from the employer to the employee specifying that the employer recognizes that the employee may need to be absent for an extended period of time. The employer should specify that he or she recognizes this possibility and therefore wishes to remind the employee of his or her rights under the Family Medical Leave Act. The letter should

be dated which starts the clock regarding the 12 weeks of job protection specified in the law. If the employer grants this medical leave without formally invoking FMLA, then the employer is inadvertently extending the protected time the employee is allowed to be gone. If the employee is out two or three weeks and then the employer invokes FMLA, the employer cannot go back and set the date starting FMLA protections from the first day the employee left. FMLA protections start on the date that the employer formally invokes FMLA protections.

4. If the employer decides that the job cannot be held open for the employee's return (prior to the end of FMLA protections) or if upon the employee's return, he or she cannot do the job as well as the employee had done prior to the leave and terminates that employee, the employer runs the risk of a wrongful discharge lawsuit. Wrongful discharge is exactly what it sounds like: the employer has wrongfully discharged or terminated the employee, and the employee exercises his or her rights to recourse in civil court.

The way this works is that the employee contacts an attorney and explains the situation asking, "Do I have a case?" The attorney says yes and then maybe suggests that the individual file a complaint with the EEOC or the state human rights commission. Neither the EEOC nor the state human rights commission costs the employee any money, so a complaint to them triggers a cost free examination. If the EEOC or the state human rights commission determines that the discharge was in violation of a law or rule, they will call for a remedy, which usually includes restitution or remuneration to the wrongfully terminated employee, and a fine (usually three times actual damages) which is paid to the EEOC or the state human rights commission. Once this is done, a civil law case will usually follow which will cost the employer additional legal fees, court costs, and perhaps additional restitution. In a situation where an employee's job is considered essential, there is a loophole in FMLA that allows the company not to hold the job open if it creates hardship for the organization. However, should the employee file a complaint regarding the loss of the job due to health-related issues, the company is held accountable to prove the job was essential.

Managing the Mess

I have a few more general, but salient, suggestions for you. As you encounter and then face a personnel mess, I would like you to consider that your first instinct is going to be fight or flight. Depending upon your bias, your instincts will tell you to "steel" yourself and take the matter head-on, or they will tell you to run "like hell." Either response is probably going to be inappropriate. Unfortunately, most management situations are counterintuitive. Your intuition will tell you to do one thing, but usually that one thing isn't going to be correct. And, management by trial and error can be very costly in money and time.

Remember the old adage: the best approach is ready, aim, and fire. If you follow your fight or flight instincts, you are probably doing the opposite and not thinking things through. It's instinct to go initially to the fast fix. What I suggest is something different. When you're faced with a management mess, your first reaction will be to formulate plan A. Plan A is usually the "path of least resistance" and something that will work in a perfect world. Sometimes, as we get into plan A, there is a need make midcourse corrections because the world isn't perfect, and things are rarely an easy fix. This we can essentially call plan B. When this plan or strategy doesn't work, we are generally left with the most radical or least attractive alternative — plan C. Plan C is that thing that we really didn't want to face as we didn't want to have to work this hard or take as much time. It's not that we want to run from our problems; it's just human nature that we hope they will solve easily and that plan A will work.

My experience tells me that plan A is related to that flight or fight response, not thought out or very realistic. As you get into plan A, which has inherent flaws, plan B emerges but it is little more than attempting to jam the round peg deeper into the square hole. Plan C will probably be the most effective way to solve the problem. Unfortunately, the activities associated with plans A and B may have so soiled the footpath, that plan C may have little chance at success. My recommendation for you is to go ahead and make plan A, even plan B. Put them down, either on paper or compose them at the keyboard. Look at them closely. Then be realistic, take a hard swallow, and set both aside. Now draft plan C.

Once you have a realistic plan, identify someone who you respect and trust. Remember that you cannot take an unpolished idea up, and you cannot vent down. If you take an unpolished idea up to your board or your boss, its flaws will be identifiable, and it will be a poor reflection on your skills and judgment. If you take your ideas to the next level down or below you in the organization, you could be creating another problem for yourself. Unless you're really careful about whom you select, communicating down can undermine your position in management. Under certain circumstances, conversing with a trusted subordinate is perfectly fine. However, if that "trusted' subordinate turns on you or acts in a predatory manner and takes the information out of context, it could undermine you.

What I'm suggesting is that you identify a mentor or, better yet, several mentors to assist you in polishing your ideas and planning your moves. Napoleon Hill, in his landmark 1937 book, *Think and Grow Rich*, urged his readers to establish what he described as a mastermind group. Abraham Lincoln, when he became President of the United States, grew to distrust his Cabinet. Due to the political realities of the times, he could not dismiss them, but he knew that he still needed trustworthy people around him. He developed what has been historically described as his "kitchen cabinet." Whether you call them a board of directors, a kitchen cabinet, or a mastermind group, I recommend that you find these people. Everyone needs an individual or, better yet, a group of individuals to assist him or her in polishing ideas and establishing plans of action.

When faced with personnel messes, you need to have the wisdom and courage to identify, and then implement plan C. You should present your dilemmas and concerns to your mastermind group and gather their inputs to gain confidence in the plans and strategies specified. Again, plans A and

B will not be good enough and, in most cases, will inhibit your ability to solve the problem. As much as you want and wish for the first plans to work, my suggestion for you is to go directly to the implementation of plan C after working with a mastermind group to help polish, clarify, and perfect it.

I have intended, using the book's cases as a springboard, to provide you with management lessons. Indeed, this has been the purpose of the book: to provide you with suggestions for best practices and solutions for very real management situations. I have believed, for many years, that inside each of us is a reservoir of information that has been gleaned from all of our experiences in dealing with problematic as well as multiple other situations. So, when an idea or situation is encountered, we travel consciously or subconsciously into that reservoir to gather the related experiences and information. Then we access and apply it.

Let me provide a personal example. I worked for a supervisor who "inherited" me. One piece of important background on this individual was that he had completed an associate's degree from a community college. While I was hired by someone else in the company, I reported to this individual and noticed pretty quickly that I was objectionable to him. I couldn't understand why this individual treated me with disdain until a friend of mine in the company asked me if I knew why my boss seemed to hate me. I was thrilled to be provided with this piece of insight. Apparently, my boss had an issue with higher education. It seems that his first wife, who had a masters, left him and subsequently married a college professor with a doctoral degree. From that point on, this individual had a very distinct and negative picture in his mind about people with a doctoral degree. I had a doctorate, and he generalized and projected his feelings onto me. He went down into his reservoir, resurrected his experience and feelings relative to people with doctoral degrees, applied those to me, and treated me with the same disdain that he had for the person to whom he lost his first wife. He was working on autopilot, and his actions and thoughts were triggered by his past marital issues, not me.

Clearly, the reservoir is a very potent part of our lives, the basis of who we are. It is as important as any other part of our body. Using the reservoir or relying on the reservoir for problem solving when a situation arises can itself be severely problematic. Why? There are lots of reasons. The information could be outdated and therefore not applicable. The information could be biased or simply wrong because we misinterpreted something in our past experience. Think back to the example of my supervisor treating me with disdain because of my degree. Are all people with doctoral degrees the same? Do they all take other people's wives? It doesn't take a genius to see the flaws in such thinking, but the impact of my supervisor's experience with a person with a doctoral degree was a very powerful influence in his life. It takes someone very strong to recognize the need to override the experiences of the reservoir. One has to be a critical thinker, an objective thinker, and basically educable regarding the present. Times change and one simply cannot continue to rely heavily on one's reservoir of experiences.

I offer another example. I have an uncle who, during the time I was in college, had a manufacturing business. He employed over 400 people, and each summer I worked for him driving a forklift. One day he saw me and called, "Hey buddy, come here, I want to speak to you. I asked, "Uncle Bob, what's this buddy thing?" He told me that he had about 300 men and about 100 women working for him, and he couldn't keep up with everybody's name so he chose to refer to all the men as buddy and all the women as honey or darling. When asked why he did that, he said, "I don't know. I think my father did that." Informing him that my name was Steve, I was his sister's oldest son, and I baby-sat his children, I made it clear that I didn't like being called buddy. I also told him (and I pointed to a female employee) that that lady over there was Dorothy, and she didn't like being called honey or darling by the company president. He told me to shut up, get back on the truck, and he would speak to my mother about my impertinence.

The lesson here is that my uncle chose to solve the problem of not remembering names by reaching down into his reservoir and drawing out the solution of using buddy or honey. Buddy isn't really offensive to me, just a bit impersonal. Being referred to as honey or darling for Dorothy, and countless other female employees, was offensive. In fact, it could be easily interpreted as sexist and therefore actionable today as part of a claim of sexual harassment.

Whether it is an issue with sexual harassment, policy, or a myriad of other situations, an organization's values are on display with every decision and act — how you handle tough situations is an important matter. Your organization's values are shown with every decision and every choice that is made. Make no mistake, the employees are watching and vicariously living with each decision. How are people treated when they make mistakes? How are people treated when they succeed? How are people fired? How is the wealth shared? Is the wealth shared? The answers to these questions all center around values.

Again, the steady state of any organization should be peace, another tenant of management. The steady state of the organization should be one of tranquility so that productivity and performance can be the priority. If there is a war or a skirmish underway, then productivity and performance will always be subordinated to the war. Management should spend its time developing performance enhancements for staff, which is essentially the coaching process. All discipline should have training at its root and should never be punitive in nature.

No doubt, you have been, or will be, faced with many of the same problems as those specified in these cases. When you encounter these situations of "sex, drugs, and rock'n'roll," you now have some management practices as well as legal and regulatory insights to help address them efficiently and effectively. Hopefully, the tools provided in this book will enable you to not only be effective at management, but to flourish as well. You're also welcome to contact me at my website: steve@oncallhumanresources.com.